WEB PAGE DESIGN

in easy steps

BRIAN AUSTIN

In easy steps is an imprint of Computer Step
Southfield Road . Southam
Warwickshire CV47 OFB . England

http://www.ineasysteps.com

Notice of Liability

Every effort has been made to ensure that this book contains accurate
and current information. However, Computer Step and the author shall
not be liable for any loss or damage suffered by readers as a result of
any information contained herein.

Trademarks

All trademarks are acknowledged as belonging to their respective
companies.

Printed and bound in the United Kingdom

ISBN 1-84078-039-8

Table Of Contents

11 Utilising 'power' components 107

12 Gaining information with online forms 119

13 Designing your Web pages 129

Creating a killer business Web site! 147

Launching, promoting and marketing 171

Index 187

Planning your Web site

Every successful venture needs a plan, so in this chapter we tackle those sometimes tricky preparation issues that you need to consider before creating your Web pages.

Covers

Chapter One

Introducing the Web

The Internet, or 'Net', is a vast collection of interconnected computers spread across the globe providing information on almost any subject imaginable. The World Wide Web (WWW) – more commonly known as the Web – is a 'branch' of the Internet and provides access to a vast amount of information through Web pages.

To learn more about the mechanics of creating Web pages, try 'HTML in easy steps'.

Through the Web, a visitor using one computer can access information on another computer which may be close by or a long distance away: location is irrelevant on the Net!

Web pages can contain text, images and other graphics, sound, video and other types of animation and are saved as files stored on thousands of computers across the globe. Related web pages 'linked' together at the same location make up a Web site; however, even a single self-contained Web page can be a Web site.

If you're new to the Internet, why not take a peek at 'The Internet in easy steps' to better understand how it all works?

'Simple' Web pages contain only some text and special codes or tags which determine how this text should appear. These codes that determine how Web pages behave are part of a simple computer language called HyperText Markup Language (HTML) and the more recent, more powerful version, Dynamic HTML (DHTML).

To learn about the Web's most popular browser, try 'Internet Explorer 5.5 in easy steps'.

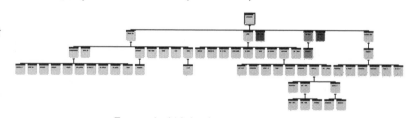

Example Web site tree structure

To create Web pages, you don't necessarily need to understand HTML as DTP-type software is now available enabling you to concentrate on how you want to design your pages rather than how to actually enter the codes to make them work. Nevertheless, to achieve complex and sometimes tricky to set up special effects, more often than not an in-depth knowledge of HTML can save you time and much 'hair-pulling'!

Creating a Web site: an overview

To create your Web site, you'll need:

- **Access to the Internet:** for most folks, this means a PC with an active modem or ISDN link and an Internet Service Provider (ISP).

- A **Web 'host'** to store and display your Web site.

- **Software** to create your site. Examples include: Microsoft FrontPage, Adobe PageMill, NetObjects Fusion and Adobe GoLive.

If you need to save money, it's possible to create HTML Web pages using most basic text editors or word processor applications.

- A Web-oriented **graphics design software** such as Paint Shop Pro, Adobe Illustrator, Photoshop or ImageReady.

- **Knowledge and skills to use the above:** books like this one can help here. For more complex animated additions, specialist skills are required.

- Several **Web browsers** (ideally) installed on your PC to check compatibility – ideally, the most recent versions of Microsoft Internet Explorer and Netscape Navigator. Or Web site validator software/checking.

- **FTP Software** to upload your Web site to your Web host when you're ready to go 'live'.

- (Optional) For businesses, **e-commerce and database** design/adaptation components.

Netiquette & the spirit of the Web

Netiquette is Internet etiquette. It's all about exercising consideration for other online users.

Avoiding the spam

No, we're not talking meat! Spamming is a quaint term used to describe the practice of sending uninvited email and news clips to vast numbers of users without their permission! This sort of activity is usually frowned upon by many amongst the Internet community. Spamming also helps clog up the Internet for all of us.

Two areas where you should not blatantly advertise products or services are amongst newsgroups and mailing lists (see Chapter 15 for more information).

Share something valuable – and gain!

Some of the most effective and eye-catching sites on the Web work well arguably because their providers are sharing something that is of real value! For example: rare, unique, valuable or useful information; an offer of free software or try-before-you-buy software; hints and tips on a particular topic; and so on. One reason why the Internet and Web are so popular is the wealth of information anyone can obtain freely or cheaply.

Computers can often present a cold, uncaring and indifferent face. You can bring warmth to a Web page by relating your message using content that is familiar to people everywhere: use sights, sounds, thoughts and feelings.

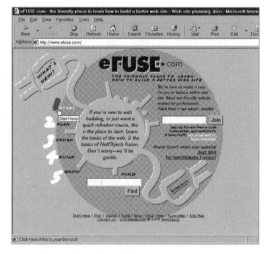

Using this approach, you can benefit by creating further incentives for people to visit your Web site. If you're hosting a Web information business and you're providing special information, you could provide some (but not all) information in a series. This is reasonable and allows visitors to decide whether it's relevant and worthwhile.

Establishing purpose

Establishing what to include and what to omit from a Web page is a crucial element in the design process. Above all, keep focused on what your Web site is for. Consider the following guidelines:

- Each Web page has a distinct purpose and a central message; always keep this in mind when designing each page.

- Create a logical hierarchy in how you display information. This presents an obvious and easy-to-understand-at-a-glance structure.

- Try to make sure a page is not too 'busy' or contains several prominent elements which fight for attention.

- Balance page components by subtle use of strong and weak colours as well as physical size and placement.

Adding fun-type animat-ions, 'production' clip art and garish colour schemes etc. to a personal Web site is a matter of personal taste. However, for a business-oriented Web site, a much more considered approach is called for (see Chapter 14 for more guidelines).

For businesses

For businesses, essentially your Web site is simply an electronic brochure that helps you. Your Web site is a funnel – a customer 'filter' to:

- Capture an email address.

- Make a new sale.

- Start a dialogue.

What you decide to include in your Web 'brochure' is one aspect. However, what you decide to leave out is probably just as important: resist the urge to include everything about a company or organisation.

Key point: the good news is, you don't need an expensively designed Web site to make money. Arguably, the less 'overwhelming' your Web site is, the more effective your Web campaign can be. Some of the most profitable Web sites have a simple structure.

Profit tip: Consider keeping back half of your Web site development budget to spend on a careful promotion and developing a considered search engine submission strategy.

Profiling your target visitor

Before you start to think about designing your Web pages, learn about who your visitors are and what type of computer technology they're likely to be using. For example, consider:

- What is their approximate age? What range of jobs do they perform? Are they young or more mature? Younger visitors might prefer a dynamic, highly colourful approach, whereas perhaps professional management consultants may identify better with a more subtle, corporate Web-type site.

- Where do they live? What language do they speak? Some would argue English is becoming an accepted international language, but even the English language has variations: American, Canadian, International and British. So this may highlight possible spelling oddities to consider. Also, be aware that some colours and colour combinations can also have special meaning in some cultures.

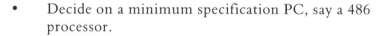

- Decide on a minimum specification PC, say a 486 processor.

- Establish which operating systems they're using.

- If you intend to use sound or multimedia, consider whether your visitors will have PCs that can process your sound files and how they may react about your Web site if they can't experience some aspects of it!

- What is the range and power of video cards used? Most PC users now by far view in at least 800 x 600 (SuperVGA) resolution instead of the older 640 x 480 (VGA). Nevertheless, don't assume this to be the case every time: still check (see the tip). And so on.

By asking questions of this type that are relevant, you can decide the level of sophistication you can safely use without alienating visitors.

Creating a design strategy

To create effective Web pages, essentially you need to complete two main tasks:

- Create HTML code that meets the current standard.

- Devise designs that are quick-loading, interesting, attractive and which are 'tuned' to the interests of your target visitors.

Sounds easy, doesn't it? Let's take a closer look.

Use off-screen planning to get started

Before setting to work with your Web page design software, put pen to paper and note down your initial ideas; what you want to achieve from your Web site.

Create an outline 'tree' structure with your Home/Index page at the top. Then create the main 'link' pages that feed off the Index page.

You can gain ideas about how to design your Web pages by seeing how other, similar Web sites appear. Note carefully what you like and dislike, then adjust your designs to create even better standards.

Arguably, one of the key reasons why so many commercial Web sites are failing, is that they have a cold corporate look and feel. Many of those who are succeeding however, get personal with prospects and customers: people are treated as individuals; warmly and with respect. So why not use this simple knowledge to build your Web success too?

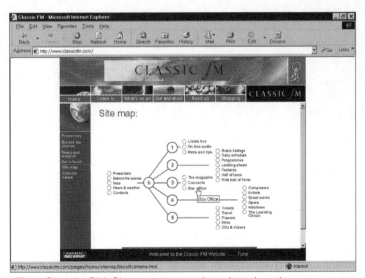

The Classic FM Sitemap page showing the site structure

Draft out the opening Web page in more detail. Aim to create a logical opening structure and try out different approaches. Keep it appropriate to your visitors. Make it inviting but simple to navigate.

14 key Web guidelines to help you succeed!

However you eventually decide to create your pages, some things are essential to know before you get down to work. Consider the following guidelines:

If your Web pages are dealing with particularly complex topics, provide information in 'bite-sized' chunks. Use (active) space to provide plenty of 'breathing space'.

- For those in business, a true domain Web page address is arguably *essential* for all sorts of reasons (see Chapter 14 for detailed guidelines)!

- The fast pace of modern living for many means that available time can be in short supply: help your visitors by making sure your pages load quickly (more about this hugely important point later).

- First impressions on the Web count. Aim to create a great impression on the first visit. Within the first 60 seconds of logging onto your Home/Index page, a visitor forms an opinion – sometimes subconsciously – about your site, and therefore about you, your company, or the organization that you represent!

If you use familiar components (like the same toolbars, fonts and tables) and follow the same information delivery plan across your pages, visitors know what to expect, and so this helps them absorb information more easily.

- When considering what to include in a Web page, usually many choices emerge. Try to put yourself in the place of a visitor and ask yourself what they would want. Make a short list, then leave out anything else not essential.

- Don't provide too many choices – this only overwhelms and confuses people. Limit page/site navigation options to between 7-10. These could be buttons, icons, individual parts of a larger image, or simply text components.

- Aim to make your Web pages attractive, compelling and engaging. This and similar books can help show you how. Create a consistent design style that does not overpower the central message.

- Carefully focus design aspects towards your target audience to ensure they can quickly identify with what you're saying or offering.

- If your Web site essentially provides information, use fast-loading graphics with your text. Unless you have a special reason, limit the use of special animation effects like Shockwave-, Flash- and Java-type content.

- If your Web site is primarily aimed at entertaining or advertising, Shockwave- and Java-type animations will probably enhance your presentation! However, always consider your visitors – and provide options. Also try to define the level of computer equipment they're likely to be using, then modify your designs to match.

Another potentially useful way to develop ideas for your Web site is to brainstorm with friends or colleagues. Each can write down initial thoughts – however wacky – then collectively discuss ideas. Finally, build a plan from the results.

- Remember, generally visitors don't like having to scroll down a page in order to read it. However, compelling sales-oriented material may be tolerated providing it's not too long (over 4 screen-lengths).

- Don't force visitors to have to scroll from left to right to read your text. Use narrow newspaper-like columns.

- Generally, visitors are not keen to read what they consider to be unnecessary material. One way around this problem is to briefly include the essential information first. Then next to this, insert links to other pages that contain the detailed information.

Fast-loading rollover links in the form of simple graphical buttons like those shown in this example can provide quick and easy access to all the essential pages in your Web site. Good quality Web design software often include pre-designed buttons ready for you to use.

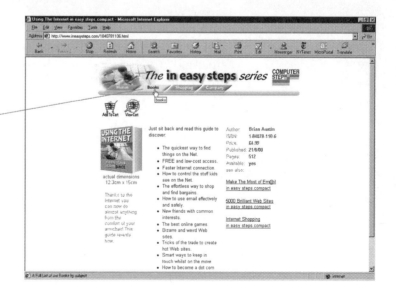

• For businesses, aim to design your entire Web operation to compel visitors to voluntarily leave their email address with you. Targeted email addresses are like liquid gold! They form the off-line equivalent of your mailing list. If you don't capture a visitor's email address the first time they visit, you may never have another chance of selling something to the email address holder. Use ezines, quizzes, competitions, draws, and so on to provide 'magnetic' variety.

Making your Web site easy to use is a priority. This doesn't mean that it has to be boring. Effective communication can be achieved through providing relevant and valuable information with carefully considered colour combinations.

• Finally, never forget the three most important reasons why visitors are 'turned off' a Web site:

— When it's boring.
— When it takes too long to load.
— When it's confusing to use.

Meeting the HTML standard

The HyperText Markup Language (HTML) is used to create working Web pages. Yet HTML is continually being developed and improved. When designing your Web pages, it's important to ensure they meet the current HTML standard and to decide how far you want to go to support earlier Web browsers. See your Web design software manuals for more details.

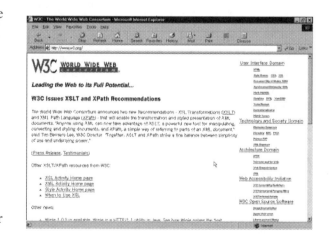

You can discover the current HTML version by pointing your browser to the World Wide Web Consortium (W3C) Web site. The W3C sets the HTML standards and is available at: http://www.w3.org/

Establishing when to stop

No one should presume to tell you when your Web page design is 'right'; only you as the designer really know that. But you can reach a stage beyond which any further contribution you make doesn't improve the result.

Lessons from the artists

How often, as children, have many of us created a drawing or painting of which we're proud, only to become so excited that we try to 'make it a little better'? By the time we realise the mistake, it's too late – the picture is spoiled. And as grownups, many professional artists providing drawing and painting workshops press home the point to their students: 'Don't overdo it', 'Know when to stop'. Some even say: 'When you think the drawing is *almost* complete, it *is* complete and that's the time to stop!'

Sometimes the desire to create something special can lead to adding complex cutting-edge features to a Web page. This may be fine, but if ill-considered can result in a 'one-browser-only' Web page – not so good for businesses. Test drive your designs with several browsers before going live.

As a Web page is essentially a graphical medium, this kind of advice can be relevant here too. As we design our pages, it's easy to become so absorbed in the process and to so enjoy it that we can sometimes lose sight of the real goal: to create an attractive, usable and interesting offering that people will want to revisit again and again.

Harnessing the power of active space

Space has power! Yes, even empty areas of a Web page can deliver a powerful message in their own right. Considered use of empty space is not really empty at all: it's active. This 'active space' adds to the overall offering. So many Web pages now are filled with pointless 'clutter' that those that are designed with economy in mind can stand out.

In conventional publishing, the power of active white space has long been accepted. In the daily newspapers, periodically we see advertisements which take up an entire page, but which might perhaps contain a single entity or small amount of carefully considered text. Yet our eyes, which arguably have not been trained to expect this in a newspaper, are drawn to the page with the result that such advertisements can be very effective in gaining our attention. We can apply this approach to our Web designs with just as much success!

Choosing your Web host

A Web host stores your pages and makes them available to visitors. Literally thousands of companies worldwide are available that you can employ to host your Web site and the one you choose need not even be located in your own country. So how do you go about choosing the one that's right for you? Consider the following 'ideal' guidelines:

- **Technical support:** 7-day, 24-hour email/live support with reply in under 24 hours – under 12 is better.

A good way to really check out the claims a Web host makes is to speak to some of their existing customers.

- **Web space:** 100 Mb will probably provide enough space for about 1000 pages; 20 Mb may be more than enough for most people.

- **Contract duration:** ideally, get a 'no minimum contract' deal so you can cancel at any time. Some offer discounts if you pay 1 year in advance.

- **Unlimited Hits:** a 'hit' occurs when a visitor views your Web page.

Visit some Web sites hosted by a Web host to evaluate their claims. Check things like speed of access and how long Web pages they host take to load, and so on.

- **Mirroring and peering:** peering and mirroring ensure your site will always provide the fastest connection speeds available.

- **Email addresses:** ideally get unlimited (or enough) email addresses so that you can create variations like: orders@yourcompany.com and support@yourcompany.com

- **Autoresponders:** Unlimited (see Chapter 14). Great for business Web sites.

- **'Downtime':** During downtime, your Web site is not visible (Example: Web hosts need to perform their own maintenance to keep things running smoothly). A good host will have 99% 'uptime' leaving 1% for downtime.

- **Cost:** Obviously the lower the better, but generally you get what you pay for!

- **CGI bin:** providing special scripts, forms, etc.

- **E-commerce capability/support:** vital for businesses.

Web page design basics

In this chapter, we learn about the basic rules and components that affect most Web pages and tackle some key issues to help you avoid possible pitfalls later on.

Covers

Chapter Two

Popular Web design tools

Often, the most attractive and appealing Web pages have benefited from the skills of professional Web page designers and graphic artists. These skills cost money, but the results can set your site apart from the crowd.

'How can I create Web pages?' A fair question. Let's tackle it. If you're feeling really brave, you can create HTML using any text editor like TextPad or Windows Notepad. However, for most folks, those tools are ideal for fine-tuning but not much help in getting your creative juices to flow. The best Web design tools now take a graphical or DTP-like approach to creating Web sites. Popular programs include:

- Adobe PageMill and its much more powerful multimedia-oriented big brother, GoLive! (www.adobe.com/products/golive/main.html).

- Dreamweaver from Macromedia (www.macromedia.com/software/dreamweaver/).

- FrontPage from Microsoft (www.microsoft.com/frontpage/).

- Fusion from NetObjects (www.netobjects.com/products/html/nf4.html).

- HotMetal Pro from SoftQuad (www.hotmetalpro.com).

Popular Web graphics tools

Wizards can do the bulk of Web page creation for you. Simply answer some basic questions and the software does the rest. You can then make final adjustments manually. Microsoft FrontPage and Publisher are two great wizard-driven applications.

Most special effects that you might want to make in Web pages can be achieved using the superb Paint Shop Pro (www.jasc.com). Or you can choose excellent tools from Adobe's range: Illustrator, Photoshop and ImageReady. Other powerful graphics tools with a strong following include Fireworks from Macromedia and CorelDRAW!

Creating animations and multimedia

You can create simple animated GIF sequences (Chapter 10) using tools like GIF Animator (www.mindworkshop.com/) or Adobe After Effects. To create high quality, fast-loading Flash animations, look at Flash 4 from Macromedia (www.macromedia.com/).

These are all powerful, fairly complex applications and so take time to learn. Once they're familiar, quality and productivity can soar providing excellent value for money.

Three types of Web page

Any Web site can be made up of three types of Web pages:

- The Home page: often the first page which a visitor sees (sometimes a Welcome page precedes this).

In this NetObjects Fusion 4.0 Web site structure map, you can colour-code page sections to make things clearer.

Throughout this book, we have included some JavaScript examples. If you use these examples, make sure you type every single character correctly, and where you see quotes, use straight quotes like this ("), not curly quotes like this ("). Ideally, spend some time learning the basics of JavaScript first.

2 Home/ Index page.

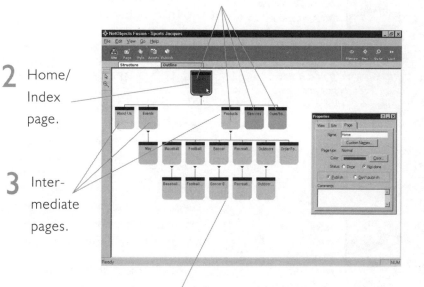

3 Inter-mediate pages.

4 Content pages can have several levels. Ideally, however, ensure that a visitor can easily move to any page within about 3 mouse clicks.

- Intermediate pages: these are the pages which are 'the next level down' immediately accessible from the Home/Index page. Usually, there's a link back to the Home page from each of these intermediate pages.

- Content pages: these contain topic details and are usually accessible from Intermediate pages. Often, Content pages may also include a link back to the Home page in addition to other relevant links.

Home | Site Home | Index | Search | Checkout

The value of first impressions

Someone once said: 'You never get a second chance to make a first impression', and on the Web this has never been more true. Here, looks and usability are everything!

When someone accesses your Web site for the first time, they don't know you – or trust you, and many people are naturally suspicious – especially in view of all the over-hyped stories that circulate in the media from time to time about the Internet.

Words provide the 'glue' that holds your Web presentation together. Nevertheless, the Web is essentially a graphical medium. So try to make your Web pages colourful, engaging, vibrant and lively.

People appreciate being considered! Be professional – a simple statement that can have big implications in your Web design (and sales, if you're in business).

There's a great tendency now on many Web sites to include as much action, animation, electronic tricks, flashing logos, graphics or icons as possible. Resist this urge and instead let the three C's dictate your overall design:

- **Consistency:** try to create a similar style of presentation across all the pages in your Web site. Visitors then know what to expect and this helps them absorb information more easily.

- **Colour:** contrast helps an item stand out or blend in.

Once you've stimulated visitors to visit your Web pages, to maintain interest update the pages regularly and let visitors know when you'll be doing this to help create a sense of expectation.

- **Content:** within the first few seconds of seeing your Home/Index page, your visitors should know the main benefits of what you're providing.

Minimising Home/Index page download time

Every second counts on the Net! You can save precious seconds by applying the careful design techniques you'll learn in this book. You may have superb content but if something causes your visitor to not wait until it has finished downloading, all your efforts are wasted.

Key point: try to ensure your Home/Index page is fully downloaded within about 25-30 seconds using a 28.8 Kbps modem – ideally within 10 seconds. Results of recent studies suggest we're getting more impatient and may move on to another Web site if we don't get sufficient visual payback within 10 seconds of the page starting to load!

Utilising the power of headlines

One of the best ways to let visitors know what you're offering quickly is with carefully worded headlines placed at the top of your pages and at other key locations.

1 Your main aim is to catch the attention of your visitor with a powerful 'what's-in-it-for-me?' question immediately answered through your headline.

2 The most important benefit of your Web site/page should be made absolutely clear in the main Home/Index page headline. It's here where you'll keep or lose a new visitor.

3 The other main benefits of your Web site, product or service can then be listed logically in your remaining headlines.

If you're successful, your visitor will probably be motivated enough to continue exploring your Web site and indeed, that is the main reason for highlighting your headlines.

On your Home/ Index page, ask your visitor to bookmark your site. Also, ask them again on several other pages, just in case they forget.

Always put strong benefits first!

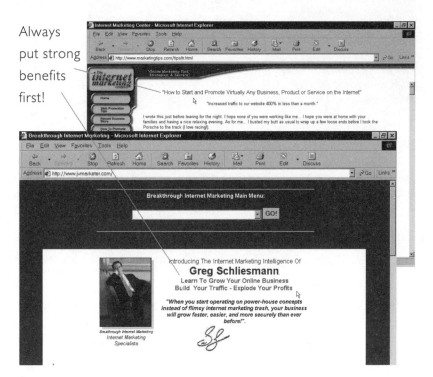

Tables: the cornerstone of design

All Web browsers support tables. A HTML table is, in its simplest form, a grid of cells laid out in rows and columns. Each table cell can contain text, numerical data, an image or even another table. Presenting information using tables is one of the simplest yet most powerful techniques available to Web designers. For example:

One way to quickly increase the size of margins in a table is to increase the padding values between columns and rows.

- Correct use of HTML tables ensures neatness and order are demonstrated over a range of browsers.

- Information can be presented in precise row and column format.

You can include any table created in a word processor-type application as a graphic object if you wish. However remember, in this event, each time you want to change information in the table, you'll probably need to edit the image in the source application and then re-insert it into the Web page.

Tables help align information and objects neatly

- A variety of attributes can be applied to your tables and their cells including: using different shades, applying or hiding borders, changing cell size, spacing and padding (empty space around a cell).

- Tables provide the illusion that text, numbers and images can be positioned independently anywhere on a Web page.

You can change the look of a table by using techniques to combine adjacent cells (spanning) and through inserting a table into the desired cell of another table. Usually, the table background takes precedence over the Web page background.

However, if no background colour is specified, the properties of the Web page usually apply.

1 Here the popular 3-column format is used.

2 Newspaper-type columns make for easier reading.

3 Colour, contrast and quality graphics bind the theme together.

4 Tables are used here to help align text, headings and graphics.

Creating fixed or variable sized tables

Your Web design software should allow you to specify the size of a table either in pixels or percentages (at least). Therefore, choose:

1 Pixels to create a table size that stays the same irrespective of the Web browser used. Benefit: you know that a table will display the same on different browsers. Drawback: if a browser window is too small, a visitor may have to scroll horizontally to view all the information.

2 Percentages when you want a visitor's browser to resize the table on the fly to match the current size of a visitor's browser window. Main drawback: as you lose control of the design, you may not know for sure how a table will appear.

Using HTML HEIGHT and WIDTH tags in your tables

Normally, Netscape browsers don't display any information within a table until all the graphics have been downloaded into the browser. However, by specifying values in the HEIGHT and WIDTH tags in HTML, you can ensure your visitors can immediately read the text in your tables while the remaining information is downloading.

If you want to display information in a precisely defined layout – like a poem for example – occasional use of the <PRE> tag in HTML provides the simplest solution.

Remember, <PRE> preserves the exact character and line spacing/ break sequences. <PRE> is also useful for creating perfectly aligned columns of text.

See your HTML guide or 'HTML in easy steps' for more information.

How Height and Width tags are shown in HTML

Using a quick loading header table to keep visitors entertained

If you insert most of the main content of a Web page within a table, sometimes a situation can develop in which the background loads first, followed minutes later by the text and graphics.

To avoid this situation, you could create a separate table containing some key information and place this at the top of your Web page.

This smaller table will then display before the main table and your visitors have something to view while the main table is downloading.

Presenting information using lists

Listed information can be displayed in HTML Unordered or Ordered list format. Let's examine the differences.

In HTML, to create an unordered type list, use the <UL> and </UL> tags. To create an ordered list, use the <OL> and </OL> tags.

Unordered lists

In HTML, unordered lists don't have a numbered sequence. Usually, bullets are used to highlight each entry. Unordered lists are ideal for displaying:

- Text without a numbered or logical sequence.

- A nonspecific sequence of events.

- List entries indented/nested within the previous item.

In Unordered lists, you can also choose whether you want disc, circle or square bullets. Here's how: add the word 'type' after the List HTML tag <LI>, you then choose whether you want disc, circle or square. For example:

To display a list of terms and their meanings on a Web page, you can use the following Definition-type list HTML tags: <DL>, </DL>, <DT>, and <DD>.

```
<UL>
    <LI TYPE=SQUARE> Line 1 with a square bullet
</UL>
```

When entered properly in HTML, this would display as:

■ Line 1 with a square bullet

Ordered lists

An ordered list provides a more structured look, ideal for:

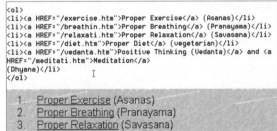

```
<ol>
<li><a HREF="/exercise.htm">Proper Exercise</a> (Asanas)</li>
<li><a HREF="/breathin.htm">Proper Breathing</a> (Pranayama)</li>
<li><a HREF="/relaxati.htm">Proper Relaxation</a> (Savasana)</li>
<li><a HREF="/diet.htm">Proper Diet</a> (vegetarian)</li>
<li><a HREF="/vedanta.htm">Positive Thinking (Vedanta)</a> and <a
HREF="/meditati.htm">Meditation</a>
(Dhyana)</li>
</ol>
```

1. Proper Exercise (Asanas)
2. Proper Breathing (Pranayama)
3. Proper Relaxation (Savasana)
4. Proper Diet (vegetarian)
5. Positive Thinking (Vedanta) and Meditation (Dhyana)

Although other list commands may be available, some browsers may interpret these commands differently. Usually, only the ordered and unordered list commands behave in the most consistent way in most browsers.

- Displaying list entries in a num-bered sequence to show a logical structure, sequence or flow.

- Indenting list entries in the same way as Unordered list entries. The numbering structure relates each entry logically to its neighbours.

Establishing ideal page width

In Web page design, the target space is the visitor's browser window. To decide the desired width (and height) of your Web pages, the topic of resolution comes into play.

Picture resolution defined

The resolution of a display monitor is the total number of pixels used to display the picture. A pixel is a single dot of light on a display monitor. The more pixels used, the better the resolution and therefore the quality of the picture. Current popular screen resolutions in pixels include:

- 640 x 480 – the older VGA standard (that is, 640 pixels wide by 480 pixels high = 307,200 pixels).

- 800 x 600 – the current popular SuperVGA standard (480,000 pixels).

- 1024 x 768 pixels – an ideal size for 19" monitors or greater (786,432 pixels).

Several different browsers and display monitor resolutions are currently available and you – as the designer – don't know which combination a visitor may be using.

Deciding on your page width

If you design your Web pages for say 800 x 600 or larger, and a visitor is viewing in 640 x 480, their browser automatically provides a horizontal scrollbar at the bottom of their browser window. To view all information on your pages, they will probably have to keep scrolling back and forth horizontally. Your visitor may decide that this is simply not worth the hassle and leave!

More users are now viewing in at least 800 x 600, and some space is taken up with the scrollbars so you won't have the full 800 pixels to use. Consider the guide below:

- 640 x 480: provides about 600 pixels of useful width.

- 800 x 600 provides about 780 pixels of useable width.

- 1280 x 1084 provides about 1200 pixels of useable width.

Establishing ideal page length

A key goal is to ensure the content of each entire Web page fits within the physical space of one screen, so visitors don't have to scroll down to find the information they want.

However, this is not always possible especially for business-oriented pages: a longer sales message can be more successful if you don't break off at a crucial moment! Consider the following general guidelines:

1 Keep your page lengths as short as possible. Try to fit all of the current topic into 1 or 2 screens.

Provide links to all the main pages in your Web site on every page and try to make sure that a visitor can get to any page in your site within 3 clicks.

2 Provide clear links to the next page in the sequence and to other related pages.

3 If you can't meet the condition is Step 1, ensure you don't force your visitors to scroll down more than 4 screen-heights as an absolute maximum.

4 To minimise the number of times a visitor has to click on the scroll buttons, and to make navigation to key parts easier, consider using index pointers included at the top or start of the Web page. An index pointer is simply any text or graphic link which, when clicked, takes the visitor to the corresponding part of the page.

5 At the bottom of each page, consider placing a link back to the index at the top of the page and links to other pages in the sequence.

For personal Web sites, micro-businesses who provide one or two products or services, and some small predominantly information-providing Web sites, sometimes it can make more sense to put everything on one carefully designed scrollable page. Ideally, observe the 4-screen-height limit to avoid irritating visitors.

Hyperlinks, buttons, icons, toolbars

A hyperlink is a link to another part of the same Web page, a separate Web page, or another Web page or location on the Internet. Hyperlinks can be made using text or a graphic object. Hyperlinks are discussed in more depth in Chapter 5. Popular graphic links use buttons and icons and may be arranged in horizontal rows or vertical columns to form navigation toolbars.

 Some of the best Web sites follow a simple design theme, with techno-logically exotic components deliberately kept to a minimum. In a highly cluttered Web, open space and simplicity often stands out.

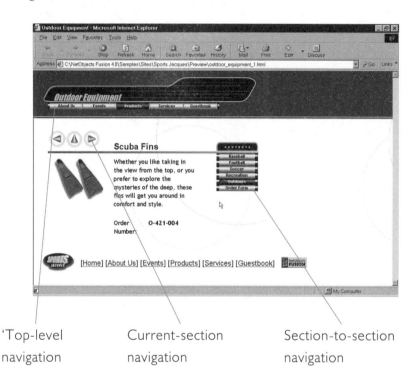

'Top-level navigation

Current-section navigation

Section-to-section navigation

Consider the following design guidelines:

• *As buttons are essentially small graphics, avoid including too much detail, and;*

• *Make the purpose of each button instantly recognizable.*

The power of a toolbar

Examples of good Web sites display a thoughtful layout and include navigation aids on *every* page – not just on the Home/Index page. A popular way of providing this feature is to use a toolbar offering a clear at-a-glance outline of the entire Web site structure.

To make the job of Web page design easier, you can buy Web page components like buttons, icons, backgrounds, and clip art especially prepared for use in Web pages. For example, see: www.webspice.com/

Traditional contact information

It's amazing how many Web sites don't include traditional contact information, like mailing address, phone and fax numbers. Web users are naturally suspicious of any new medium like the Internet, and not including basic familiar contact information does not help ease that feeling in many.

To have your email sent to one address and pre-sorted, you can use email address variations.
For example: all emails sent to 'orders@yourdomain .com' are sales, while those sent to 'feedback@yourdomain.com' all relate to feedback messages, and so on.

1 Appreciate that it is essential to provide clear and correct basic contact information if you want people to contact you. Some people may prefer to use phone or fax instead of email.

2 Include as many different contact methods as possible in your Web site – ideally: mail address (company name), contact person, phone, fax, and email.

3 Consider including contact details on all Web pages that make up your site to ensure that visitors always have immediate and easy access to contact you for more information or order goods or services.

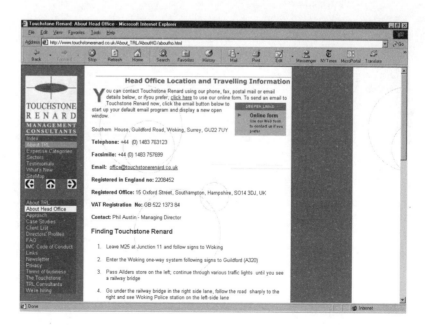

Advert banners and buttons

On the Web, page banners are everywhere! Essentially, they're the Web equivalent of TV advertisements. Banners can be animated or static, small just like buttons, or take up most of the page width. You can create a banner advert as an animated GIF image (Chapter 7) or by inserting some HTML code where you want the banner to appear.

If you want to use high quality photos in a banner, you can convert the images to JPEG format and use simple JavaScript to create an animated banner.

1 Attractive invitation.

2 Good colour contrast.

3 Clear call to action.

Guidelines:

1 Banners usually slow down the loading of a Web page.

Banner exchange banners placed at the top of a page can be indexed by a search engine before it finds your own page information. This will almost certainly cause the search engine to reduce your ranking.

2 To avoid creating too many conflicting elements or making a page too 'busy', avoid placing banners larger than 468 x 60 (pixels) and limit the quantity to a maximum of 2 per page.

3 Usually, it's best to avoid placing advertisement banners at the top of a page: a new visitor is being prompted to click on the banner and possibly move away from your site – even before reading the current page. Instead, place banners at the bottom of a page.

4 To properly assess the success of a banner, you need to measure the 'Clickthrough' and 'Conversion' rates over an extended period of time. Clickthrough rates how many clicks a banner receives. Conversion measures how many people bought as a result of clicking a specified banner.

5 Try to ensure a banner colour scheme does not clash with your page colours and make sure there's adequate colour contrast between the two.

Installing an email link on a page

Email is one of the easiest ways for your visitors to contact you. Arguably, most visitors already have a default email program installed and set up on their PC. Consider other advantages:

- Sending an email costs a fraction of what it costs to send an equivalent mail letter.

- An email can be received in seconds.

- Time zone and physical location differences become irrelevant. We can collect email when it's convenient to us.

- We don't have to be present to receive email.

Here's how email works. Each recipient 'rents' a storage area called an email box on a powerful PC (mail server). The user can then periodically examine his or her email box and download any desired messages.

To include an email link on a Web page, perform the following steps:

1. You can easily include an email link on your Home page and optionally every other page in your Web site. Usually, this is a simple operation using DTP-like Web design software. The resulting HTML looks something like this:
   `<A HREF="mailto:brian@yourcompany.com">Send Mail</A>`

2. Here, we've gone one step further. In the example below, when a visitor clicks on the 'Send Mail' link, their email program should open a new email window addressed to brian@yourcompany.com with 'Mail Me' pre-entered into the Subject field (key point: notice the exact placement of the question mark in the following example):
   `<A HREF="mailto:brian@yourcompany.com?Subject=Mail Me">Send Mail</A>`

A visitor can then quickly and easily enter their email message and click their Send button. Note: for MAILTO to work, your relevant Web pages must first be published to your Web space.

Introducing DHTML and CSS

Dynamic HTML or DHTML is essentially the latest version (v4.0) of the language that is used to create Web pages: HTML. DHTML is HTML that is made more dynamic by enabling it to work with JavaScript (Chapter 10). DHTML is, as you might expect, much more powerful and can make Web pages much more animated and interactive. For example, using DHTML, company logo components can be merged in from various directions to quickly form the complete logo in the centre of the page. Or text/graphics can fly in or off of the screen in various ways.

If you include DHTML components in your Web pages, visitors using earlier browsers – for example: Netscape v3.02 – will not be able to view your DHTML pages. However, statistics show that most users now surf the Net using v4, or later, browsers.

Elsewhere in this book, I've stated that it's important to include a textual description for each graphic used. You could also consider providing a text-only version of your Web site, or perhaps include equivalent text descriptions of all graphics used, towards the bottom of your Web pages.

When the page loads, the logo parts...

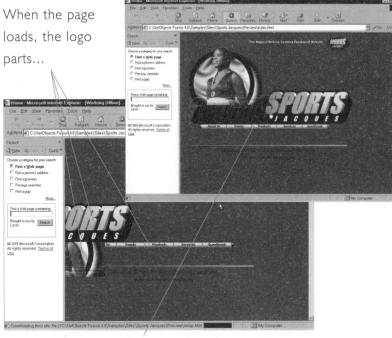

... fly in from the side to merge into a single image seamlessly

Channel Definition Format = Push technology

Channel Definition Format (CDF) (Active Channels); another development. With the usual HTML-based pages, a Web designer creates a 'channel' and CDF document. Visitors can freely 'subscribe' to a specific channel and receive regular bulletins. Updates can be downloaded to a visitor's hard drive for off-line viewing when convenient.

It's easy to become carried away with DHTML special effects.

However, these usually work best when applied carefully so as not to overwhelm a Web page, or risk taking your visitors' attention away from the main message of your page.

In raw HTML, you may often see theses symbols: <!-- and --> with some HTML or text inserted inside. These are 'comment' symbols and hide the style sheet from older browsers that cannot understand Cascading Style Sheets (CSS).

You can discover much more about CSS at the W3C web site.

Point your browser at: http://www.w3.org/Style/css/

Cascading Style Sheets (CSS)

CSS is an extension of HTML. A Cascading Style Sheet provides you with a way to control many Web page text- and spacing-related parameters at once and so save a lot of re-editing time on larger Web sites. CSS comes in three varieties: embedded, linked and inline:

- **Embedded CSS**: here a block of CSS is inserted at the start of a page to control how the page is displayed.

- **Linked CSS**: uses a .css document and other HTML pages are then linked to it. The .css document controls the look of the pages to which it is linked. By editing the .css document, you can change the look of all the pages that are linked to it. With hundreds or even thousands of pages linked to a .css page, as you can imagine this approach can save a lot of time and effort.

- **Inline CSS:** provides a way to change a single HTML tag and so allows you to fine-tune your designs.

Below is an example of embedded CSS. This is placed between the <HEAD> and </HEAD> tags in a HTML document:

```
<STYLE>
<!--
BODY {font-family: Times New Roman, Serif; color: black;}
H1 {font-family: Verdana, Arial, Helvetica; font-size: 150%; color: green;}
H2 {font-family: Verdana, Arial, Helvetica; font-size: 120%; color: green;}
TABLE {border: opx solid black; padding: 4px;}
TD.head {background-color: #808080;}
.verdana{font-family: Arial, Sans-serif;}
-->
</STYLE>
```

Note: CSS is supported in the following Web browsers and all later versions: Microsoft Internet Explorer v3.+ and Netscape Navigator v4.+

Installing a hit counter

A hit counter records the number of times a page is visited. If you use a conventional hit counter, its position is determined by the HTML code, so you place it as you would any other graphic element. However, a page counter makes a page load a little slower.

In a multi-page Web site, it's also possible to have several counters on different pages, but each would need a different reference in your HTML code.

The counter design can be simple or ornate and through varying the design in relation to the rest of your Web page, you can make a counter stand out, or ensure it takes a minor role by blending it in with the page content.

Deciding whether to include a hit counter

Sometimes, displaying a hit counter can be more trouble than its worth. Consider:

- If your pages do not receive a lot of visitors, you're advertising this fact to everyone. For a personal Web site, this may not be a problem. However, for a business-oriented site, low hit counts, perhaps unfairly, suggest a below-par business.

- Alternatively, if you have a high number of hits to your site, visitors may doubt your claims and perhaps not believe the figures are genuine and therefore assume that you have artificially inflated the figures.

Installing a Web page counter

If you decide to include a hit counter, talk to your Internet Service Provider. Some will install a counter for you. Although you can include the HTML code for your counter, because a counter integrates with your Internet Service Provider's Web servers, they may also need to carry out some set up work. Liaise closely with them.

Ideally, opt for software such as WebTrends or WebLog that tracks the number of hits discreetly, so that only you have access to the true figures, plus other key information such as visitor locations, browser types used, and so on.

Avoiding dead URL links

A dead URL link is a link to another Web address that no longer exists or to a page that has been moved. Daily, thousands of Web pages are being modified, updated, moved, reopened and closed. If you include links to other Web addresses in Web pages, before publishing your pages to the Web, make sure all such links are still correct. You can then make any changes necessary before publishing or updating your Web pages.

Once your Web site is active, regularly check the validity of your Web links, to avoid irritating your visitors with a: *'This page can no longer be found'* message.

A 'Page Not Found' error message is something to avoid. There are few other events that annoy visitors more than being asked to click on a link that subsequently leads to nowhere!

Make sure all your URLs are up-to-date and valid.

Savvy organisations go much further by providing active help and making helpful suggestions if a page address you enter is no longer valid.

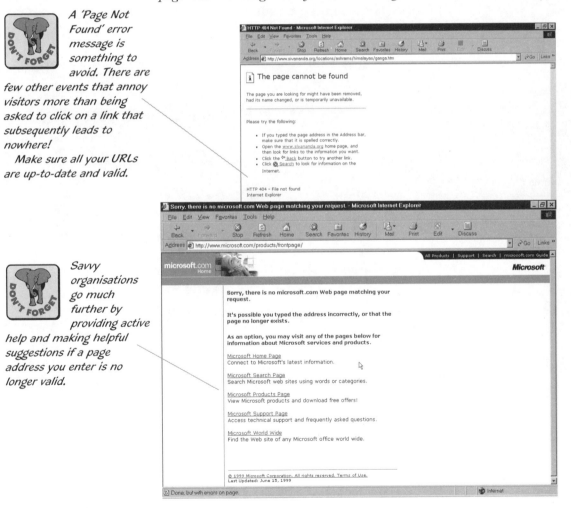

Updating your pages regularly

Once a visitor has viewed your Web site – and likes it – one of the best ways to keep your visitor coming back again and again is to update your site with new fresh content – and make sure that people know that you're updating your pages regularly. If you have carefully provided what your visitors want, updated information that is valuable to them gives them a firm reason to revisit your Web site.

You can use a 'What's New' section as the focus point for your updates. You can also let previous visitors know when your site has received important updates: simply send them an email, but get their permission to do this first ideally using an option or check box on one of your online forms, or simply send an email and ask.

While looking for fresh content to keep your pages up-to-date, try to think up new ways in which you can further your aims. For example, here a Virus Alert page provides a perfect marketing opportunity.

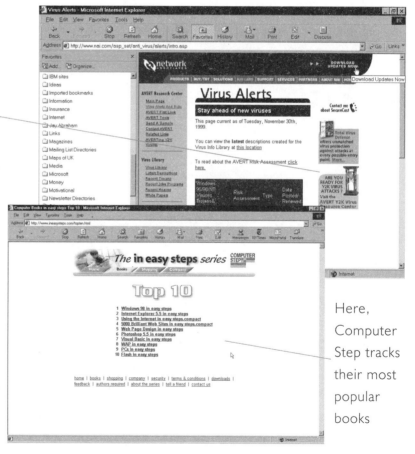

Here, Computer Step tracks their most popular books

Establishing your Web page background

The colour and type of background you choose for your Web pages make a big difference to the impact your Web site makes. Here, we list the options and examine the benefits and drawbacks of using various backgrounds.

Covers

Chapter Three

Background: exotic or plain

The kind of background used for a Web page affects the readability of text more than any other design aspect. Always ensure that there is adequate colour contrast between text and the Web page background.

If you want to use a plain light-coloured background but feel pure white is too 'clinical' for your Web page content, consider creating an off-white colour to considerably improve the warmth factor and help make screen reading less dazzling.

Most people find that black text placed on a white or light background is easiest to read. Perhaps our eyes have become conditioned through books and newspapers. Whatever you decide, consider carefully any change in your Web design that might interfere with legibility.

One of the most difficult combinations in which to achieve adequate contrast lies in using coloured text on a coloured background. Early browsers display a plain grey background; this is still the default for some AOL browser users! Most newer browsers default to white. Therefore, always specify a background colour using the BGROUND HTML tag. For example, the hexadecimal value – shown by the hash symbol # – of FFFFFF is pure white: <BODY BGCOLOR = "#FFFFFF">

Reading from a computer monitor demands more from the eye than when reading from paper-based documents. Don't use colour combinations that make reading harder, such as: medium-dark coloured text on a darker background.

You should decide what type of background is *appropriate*, bearing in mind the general content, image types and other components you want to overlay.

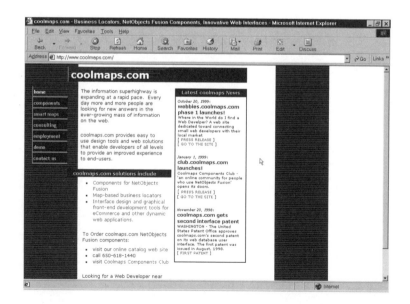

Pure black: a special approach

Carefully done, a black background can be a powerful design trait to include in your Web page. Black enhances the sense of space and depth to a Web page. However, the use of such a large expanse of black needs careful consideration and good design skills to succeed. Unless you're adept at this, usually stick to the more traditional presentation models of darker text on a lighter background.

It may sound obvious but black backgrounds can work well for products that have black associated with them. For example, black has been used in the Guinness Web site to create a stunning backdrop.

Coloured text on a black background

Generally, we don't like to read a lot of text on a conventional screen: our eyes have to work harder than when reading from, say, paper. Recent studies also suggest that most people are not comfortable with white (or light coloured) text on a black background. However, yellow text on a black background provides excellent colour contrast.

Images placed on a black background

Images placed on a black background can look impressive OR dreadful. If an image has not been designed for a black background, the results may be poor. However, when done properly then the results can be stunning. For example, the black space used in the example below compliments the product brand perfectly.

A 'poorly designed' image tends to look worse on a black background, than when laid on a lighter shade (or white) background.

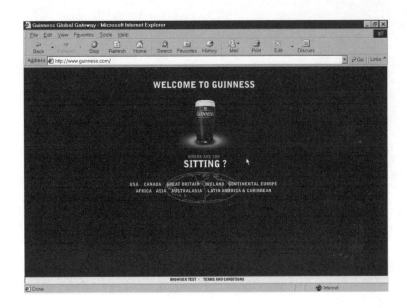

Creating a picture background

A strong picture background probably works best in Web pages which contain limited amounts of text or pages which contain primarily graphical components.

Sometimes, a Web page can be enhanced by using a single picture as the basis for the background. For this technique to succeed, consider the following points:

- The HTML standard must be version 3.0 or later. Use the <BODY BACKGROUND> HTML tag (see below).

- To ensure the picture is automatically tiled by the browser the image should be smaller than the browser window.

If you decide to use an image in your page background, always still specify a background colour so that those who turn images off see the colour you intend.
Use the HTML <BGCOLOR> tag for this (note: use the American spelling of 'colour').

- To ensure the background does not overpower overlaying text, you can convert the image to a light coloured watermark-type graphic.

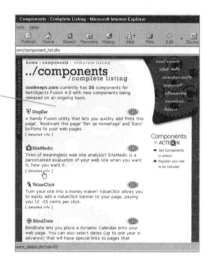

Embossing an image tones it down yet ensures that the essentials of the picture are still visible without interfering with the clarity of overlaid objects.

Creating a static background image

Normally, when you scroll down a page in a browser, the contents move up. You can, however, arrange for the background to remain stationary. Here's how:

The effect on the right usually works only in Microsoft Internet Explorer browsers, not Netscape.

1 A 'standard' HTML background tag looks like this:
   <BODY BACKGROUND="your_image.gif">

2 Add the BGPROPERTIES tag like this:
   <BODY BACKGROUND="your_image.gif"
   BGPROPERTIES="FIXED">

Creating compelling text content

Words can make or break a Web site. The look and style of text also have implications for your visitors. Here, we examine some of the best ways to create and display your text content.

Covers

Chapter Four

Providing what your visitors want

By ensuring your visitors know what to expect when they reach your Home/Index page, you can immediately build a temporary bond of trust – most people will suspend judgement until they get to know you better.

However, if your visitors expect to find information on a specific page but only find advertising, they may become irritated and start to lose faith in your site! For businesses, this is obviously bad news.

Make sure the text content of your Web pages provides the *essential* points you want to put across: don't rely on graphical components to do this as some visitors may turn off graphics in their browser.

Ensure that each Web page can stand on its own and still make sense to visitors.

Be brief, simple, direct and sincere

Remember, most folks generally prefer to read long stretches of text from paper rather than from a display monitor. Therefore, consider the following guidelines:

One way to help ensure your Web pages display within an acceptable time, is to try and ensure the text content on each page is limited to fewer than about 600 words.

You can make your Web pages printer-friendly by ensuring that the page width is not too wide (say under 550 pixels).

Experiment with different widths to ensure your visitors can view essential information when a page is printed.

1 Keep your text content short, simple and relevant, using unambiguous words and phrases rather than long stretches of text. Use lots of surrounding space to frame text blocks.

2 Provide information in concise bursts: use short paragraphs of say 5 or 6 lines maximum.

3 Borrow ideas from the newspaper industry: consider using columns no wider than about 7 or 8 centimetres.

4 For longer sections of text, consider providing a brief introduction or outline, then include a link to the full version on another page. Visitors can then choose what they want quickly.

5 Read, then re-read each line of text and remove all redundant words and phrases.

Working with fonts/typefaces

A font or typeface is a lettering style. You can choose which fonts you want to use in your pages, but for *all* visitors to see your fonts instead of theirs, those same typefaces usually need to be installed on their PC. A quick remedy is to design your pages using only fonts that are included as part of Microsoft Windows or the Apple Mac:

Text components take up the least amount of file space compared to graphics, animation and other Web page elements.

- Arial, Courier, Times Roman (for Windows PCs).

- Helvetica (for Apple Macs).

Also, Microsoft have created two excellent fonts that are specially designed for easier reading on Web pages: Verdana and Georgia are freely available for download from www.microsoft.com/ if they are not already included as part of your PC's operating system.

Using colour and headings for exposure

For cultures that read from left to right, body text is usually considered easy to read if aligned vertically at the left margin (left justified). Centred or right-justified text may be fine for the odd heading if used sparely. Experiment; try out several different combinations.

In HTML, you can specify heading sizes easily: H1 (largest size), H2 (slightly smaller), and so on. For added contrast, consider using a different colour either for body text or headings.

Entering special characters

Often, you'll need to insert special characters and symbols that HTML reserves for its own use like the HTML 'open tag' (<) and the ampersand (&) symbol. Also you may need characters that are not normally available from the keyboard, like the copyright symbol (©). If your Web design software does not provide an easy way to enter these, simply type the symbols you want between an ampersand (&) and a semicolon (;) symbols. For example:

- Less-than symbol (<), type: <

- Copyright symbol (©), type: ©

Top tips for working with text

1 Ideally, keep to no more than three different font styles unless you have a compelling reason to include a fourth. Too many fonts can create a disjointed, 'ransom note' effect.

2 Headings: to provide contrast and clarity, consider using a non-serif-type font, like Arial, Verdana, Helvetica or Georgia. Non-serif fonts don't have tails on letter edges.

3 Main body text: consider using a serif typeface – one in which the edges of letters have tails – like Times Roman. Serif fonts are easier to read at smaller sizes on a PC screen.

4 However, experiment! Consider using one of the new non-serif fonts like Verdana for your main body text in size 10p. At the smaller fonts sizes, Verdana and Georgia can excel.

5 To use a non-standard, exotic or unusual font, convert each desired text phrase/heading to a GIF, JPEG, PNG graphic (see Chapter 7 for information on how to convert).

6 Use the HTML Underline text formatting tag (<UL>) sparingly to avoid confusion. Visitors may expect underlined text to be a hypertext link. To add emphasis to text, consider using *italics* or boldface formatting instead.

7 Try to make headings and subheadings make sense at a glance so visitors can scan information more quickly. Use several words to create a better description if necessary.

Working with hyperlinks

What gives the Web its enormous power is the ability to link to other pages and Web sites anywhere. In this chapter, you can learn how to create text and graphical links between your pages and other Web sites.

Covers

Chapter Five

Text and graphical hyperlinks

A hyperlink is a link to another page or location in your Web site or to another page or location on the Web. You can create links with text or graphics. In fact, icons (small graphics) and buttons make ideal graphical links as they're usually physically small, optimised for the Web and so can load quickly in a visitor's browser.

Many Web designers choose not to place the main site links at the right side of the page. However, for most search engines, this is THE ideal location, as they don't need to navigate through non-essential items and possibly JavaScript before finding the important text for the current page.

1 In this example, when the mouse is placed on a hyperlink button....

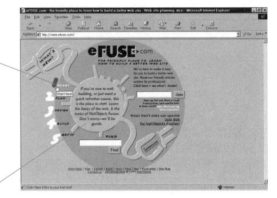

2 ... the text here changes to illustrate what the active button refers to.

Whatever tool you use, a text HTML hyperlink usually takes the following basic form:

<A HREF="http://www.websitename.com/page.html"> Click here</A>

In the above example, a visitor would see only the words 'Click here' usually underlined in blue to indicate a hyperlink. If you provide carefully considered links in your Web site, visitors don't have to use their browser Forward and Back buttons. Consider the following guidelines:

1 Ideally, place the main links to all other pages in your site at the top, left, bottom or right of the page.

2 Make sure text hyperlinks especially are clearly visible against the page background. In later versions of HTML, you can change the look of text hyperlinks (see the facing page).

Creating hyperlinks that don't have underlines

Normal HTML hyperlinks are usually coloured blue and are underlined. If you want to be more creative, you can use CSS (page 35) to create text links that are not underlined:

1 Between the <HEAD> AND </HEAD> HTML tags of your page, type in the following script.

2
```
<STYLE TYPE="text/css">
<!—
a {text-decoration: none}
—>
</STYLE>
```

In this Web page from Coolmaps.com, the 'detailed info' links, although still coloured blue, have their underlines removed

🔺 **PopRocket**
Setup a Text or Graphic link to a pop-up window. Also open and close a window on MouseOver and MouseOut.
[detailed info]

🐾 **RandomActs**
Display a random image on your page. Set images and associated links. Can also rotate images in a specified order and a specified time interval!
[detailed info]

✳ **RollOver 4.0**
Completely rebuilt for 4.0. Options include custom rollovers, status bar messages, alt tags, delays, multiple external targets, and smart highlights.
[detailed info]

Creating a JavaScript Back button

Here's a neat way to place a Back button on a Web page. (Note: this may not work on some especially early browsers):

1 Move the HTML text insertion point to the location on the page where you want to place the Back button.

2 Insert the following JavaScript code:
```
<FORM METHOD="POST">
<INPUT TYPE="button"
VALUE=BACK
OnClick="history.go(-1); return true;">
</FORM>
```

Creating hyperlink page bookmarks

Sometimes, you may want to provide a link to another location on the same Web page, rather than to another Web page or another location on the Net. You can do this by installing a bookmark (or intra-page) link. Here's how:

You can also open new windows using JavaScript. See your JavaScript guide for details. You can also learn more about JavaScript by reading 'JavaScript in Easy Steps'.

1 Place the insertion point where you want to create your bookmark and give the location a name in HTML. Example:
<A NAME="pagetop"></A>

2 Now move the insertion point to where you want to place your link then add the other half of the bookmark code:
<A HREF="#pagetop">Top of page.</A>

When a user clicks on 'Top of page', they are returned to where the 'pagetop' bookmark has been created.

Example:

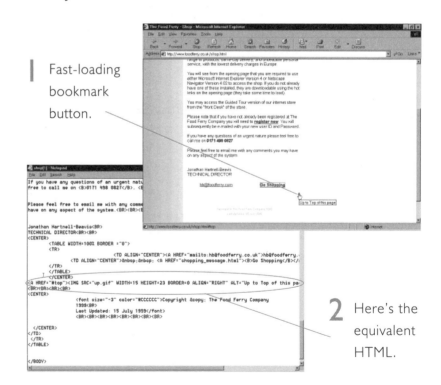

1 Fast-loading bookmark button.

2 Here's the equivalent HTML.

Linking without losing your visitor

Using a normal link, once a visitor clicks a link to move to a new Web page, the usual way they can return to your Web site would be to click the browser Back button.

On many occasions, you may still prefer to keep your Web site easily available to your visitor for marketing purposes, and so forth. Web design tools like NetObjects Fusion provide easy access to commands (target=NewWindow) that enable you to arrange for a new browser window to open overlaid on the current Web site page window.

1 In this example, if this link is clicked...

2 ... a new browser windows displays.

By arranging your design to open a second browser window, the 1st browser window stays visible and available, maintaining the original link.

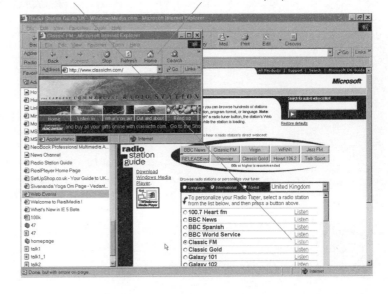

This snippet usually works on a 'live' Web page. Edit the text into your page and publish it to the Web to test.

Creating a link to open a visitor's mailbox

Add the following snippet of code to provide a link on a page that when clicked can open a visitor's mailbox (this should work fine on most recent Web browsers):

```
<A HREF="mailbox:Inbox">Click To Open Your Mailbox</A>
```

You could replace the text: 'Click To Open Your Mailbox' with a graphic icon or button if you prefer.

Linking back to the Index page

After perhaps navigating six or seven 'hops' from your Home page, a visitor might not appreciate having to backtrack the same way to return to your Home/Index page. Therefore, always include a link back to your Home page on all other pages in your Web site. Doing this also provides visitors with a standard point of reference: if they get lost, they know how to get back to 'the beginning' with a single click.

While viewing a page in your Web site, visitors may suddenly decide to contact you. You could make it easy for them to do this by including a link to your 'Contacts' page or section on every page in your Web site.

Provide a clear text or button link. Place it at a logical location

Sending visitors to a new Index page

Often, you may create a new Web site while still keeping the 'old' Web site operational for a while until you're sure everything is working fine with the new site. In this event, you'll probably want to redirect visitors who access the old Home/Index page to the new site Home/Index page.

In our example below, the new imaginary Web site address we want to redirect visitors to is:
http://www.yourcompany.com/newpage.htm

In this example, we've arranged for a visitor to be redirected to the new page in 5 seconds (CONTENT=5). If you want a different value, simply change this number.

1 In the 'old' Home/Index page, add the following code between the <HEAD> and </HEAD> tags:
<META HTTP-EQUIV="Refresh" CONTENT="5" URL="http://www.yourcompany.com/newpage.htm">

2 For the 'URL=...' section in Step 1, substitute with your new Web address.

3 Also include a normal text link to the new page for browsers that do not support the tag in Step 1.

4 Save the updated page, publish to the Web and test.

Working with related Web sites

Providing a link to other Web sites might not, at first, seem like an effective way of enhancing your own Web pages. However, this method can be a very effective way to increase your Web site's ranking in the search engines.

Let's assume you provide a Web site selling books. You could include a link to another online store that sells videos and music CDs. Imagine a music celebrity has just published their sizzling autobiography; after customers have ordered their book on your Web order form, they could also easily gain access to our celebrity's most popular videos/CDs simply by clicking the associated link.

Three or more Web sites could even work together to provide special deals for customers and to help boost their own individual product sales.

Customers benefit by having access to a better service and quick access to related subjects should they choose to follow these up. Likewise, the video Web site provider could include a complementary link to the bookseller's Home page. Both Web providers can benefit from new visitors. Here's one strategy to consider:

1 Locate names of complementary organisations that you would like to be associated with. Search engines can be useful here to find exact Web addresses.

2 Contact each of these chosen sites, send a brief email to the Webmaster introducing yourself, your Web site and your proposal. Mention that in return for them including a link to your Web site, you will include a link to theirs.

FFA (Free-For-All) pages are provided by other Web sites who let you announce your Web page address for free. In return, they get more visitors to their site.

3 If agreement is reached, you can include an eye-catching attractive link either on a dedicated 'Other links' page, or another appropriate page.

4 Try to win some Web site awards – or create your own Awards page.

5 Consider adding your Web site address to as many Free For All (FFA) pages as you consider appropriate.

Top Tips for superb linking!

Creating a hyperlink in HTML is not difficult. However, creating a linking structure that is simple, efficient and pleases both your visitors and the search engines is more challenging. Consider the following tips:

LinkBot is a service that can check all the links in your site. To discover more, point your browser at: www.linkbot.com/

1 Use HTML tables to align your links neatly on the page.

2 Make sure all links are correct, work properly and are up-to-date.

3 Make your site easy to navigate on all pages. Ideally, create a familiar style that visitors can immediately identify with.

4 Don't force visitors into a specific way of navigation: provide several alternative pathways and let your visitors decide the route.

5 Don't rely on graphical links only. Provide equivalent text and links on each page (also used by search engine spiders).

6 Remember, visitors may enter your site via pages other than your main access pages: provide hierarchical links so that your visitors can move to any other page in your site using fewer than four mouse clicks.

7 If your site has many pages – say over 50 – consider adding a Sitemap page to help visitors quickly find their way.

8 To create a link that does not have the default underline, add the STYLE="text-decoration:none" attribute to the tag. For example:
<A HREF="http://yourcompany.com/special.html" STYLE="text-decoration">Click Here for the Special</A>

The considered use of colour

Colour is everywhere. Colour is awesome. It can bring things to life, entice us, steal our attention, trigger pleasurable emotional responses or make us reel with disgust! Use of colour in your Web site is governed by the same rules. Let's explore what we can do with colour to make your Web pages a runaway success!

Covers

Chapter Six

Colours and colour combinations

Perceptions about colour

Different colours can mean different things to different people. Or you could argue that most people don't really care that much about colours used in a Web page, so long as the overall effect is clear and 'pleasing to the eye'. However, colours are used as labels and some colour combinations have special significance in some cultures. So it pays to think about the colours you use. Consider the following:

Be especially careful with the use of the HTML <BLINK> tag combined with red text. This is an alarming combination: make sure that is what you want to achieve.

- Red and yellow can be considered attention-getting, exciting or warning-type colours.

- Green inspires hope and renewal and is a reliable, relaxing, earthy colour closely associated with life.

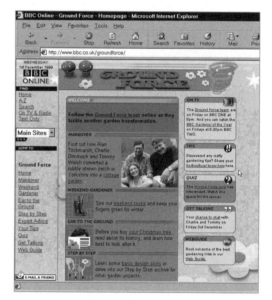

Bathed in a rich variety of greens, the BBC's Ground Force page creates a stunning presentation

Color Schemer (note the American spelling of 'colour') is a new low-priced shareware product that lets you try out different colour mixes, and helps you choose combinations that work well together on the Web. For more information, visit: www.colorschemer.com/

- Strong blue is often linked to the word trust, providing a hint as to why we so often see blue used in corporate stationery. Blue can also be considered cold, calm or tranquil depending on the intended mood.

- Black can suggest space or contrast. White can also help create the illusion of space and is often linked to cleanliness, sterility, purity or innocence.

- Purple or magenta can evoke a rich, regal tone.

Creating adequate contrast

A colour may be considered 'bright', but when it's overlaid on another the perception may be entirely different. Good contrast between a coloured object and the colour of the space surrounding it is an essential aspect for clear Web page design.

If you're developing a new adventurous Web colour scheme, get feedback from others (at an early stage) to gauge opinions on how it is accepted.

| Here, simple black text on a white background with lots of white space helps draw the eye inwards.

2 Reverse contrast helps frame the centre.

Thinking about the colour of text

Results of recent scientific legibility studies have shown that, when reading, most people prefer to view black text on a white background. White text placed on a black background is often considered the least preferred option as it is generally held to be the environment in which text is hardest to read – especially on a display monitor.

However, this combination may work better when keeping to larger typeface sizes of the sort used for headings, or text blocks which include only a few words. Perhaps the best advice is to produce your own trial pages and examine closely the issue of text legibility, particularly in relation to text colour and background combinations.

Top web colour hints and tips

Most display monitors can now display a minimum of 256 colours – 40 of which are used by the PC's operating system, leaving 216 'safe' colours.

A colour from the 216-colour palette will always display correctly using Microsoft Internet Explorer, Netscape Navigator and other compatible browsers on all current operating systems.

1 Develop a colour scheme that does not interfere with the main message of your Web page and use it consistently.

2 If you want to define your own colours, ideally keep to the 216-colour palette (see the DON'T FORGET tip), but keep to 256 colours (or greater) for photos.

3 Avoid overusing colour. The best way to meet this goal is to have a concrete reason for using each colour.

4 Use adventurous colour combinations with care. Bright neon green on bright orange makes quite an impact on the eye. This may be fine if your visitors might expect such a combination at your Web site, but is less likely to be suitable for an information-dominated Web site.

5 Consider carefully whether you should use more than 2 or 3 colours for your main body text and headings.

6 An attention-grabbing colour can only grab attention if used selectively. Setting all the body text in red lessens the impact red makes. Instead, carefully choose key words or short phrases for highlighting.

Some argue that specific Web site colour combinations – like neon green on a purple backdrop, for example – can cause headaches amongst some viewers.

7 Colour is a kind of signpost. Use colour in a consistent way, so visitors soon get to know what a specific colour on your Web site means. This concept is particularly important for navigation links, etc.

8 Consider those visitors who might be colour-blind. A colour-blind visitor may become one of your most lucrative customers, but only if he or she can see what you're offering. Red and green appear the same to colour-blind folks. Create clear colour contrast between text/background.

Creating stunning Web graphics

Pictures, images and photos can add interest and attraction to a Web page. Often, the most striking Web pages use carefully designed images. This chapter introduces current Web image formats and explains how to create stunning Web images.

Covers

Chapter Seven

Introducing Web graphics

'A picture speaks a thousand words'; on the Web, carefully considered pictures, graphics and animations can do just that. You can enrich a plain Web page with maps, cartoons, diagrams, photographs and attractive button-type icons for site navigation and other purposes. Navigation toolbars are particularly popular. However, images must be converted and optimised before use on a Web page to ensure they load quickly and can be viewed by your visitors. Current types of Web image are examined in the following pages.

Some Internet Service Providers include access to image libraries that you can use to enhance your Web pages. Check with your particular Provider. Also, some generous Web site contributors make Web images freely available for anyone to download.

How your display monitor creates an image

An image on a monitor is made up of thousands of dots of light or pixels. Many current display monitors can fill an area 800 pixels x 600 pixels resolution, which means 800 pixels wide by 600 pixels high. Other common resolutions include the older 640 x 480 and 1024 x 768 now more common on larger screens.

Some logo designs may include text content that may appear too small on a display monitor, and so not all logos may be appropriate for use on a Web page without some sort of modification.

1024 x 768 pixels

800 x 600 pixels

640 x 480 pixels

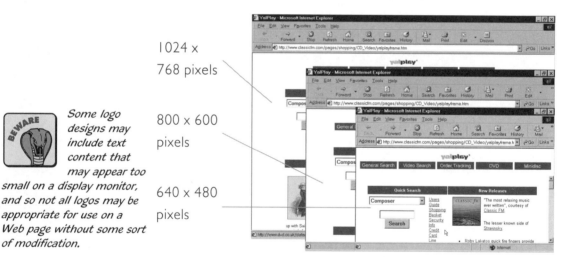

Creating simple navigational aids

Lots of attractive, interesting and complex images are available. But for site navigation and page layout, simple graphics are usually the best choice. A horizontal rule, for example, is an ideal fast-loading layout aid to use when you want to separate blocks of text by subject matter or topic.

Web image types

All sorts of graphics can be included in a Web page. A wide range of image types are available for use in documents. You may have heard of terms like BMP, CGM, PCX, TIF, WMF, GIF, JPG, the more recent development PNG and so on. So for example the file SEASCAPE.JPG tells us that the seascape image is a JPG-type image.

Although pictures help make a Web page more interesting, they can also help break down the language barrier for visitors whose native language is not your own.

Usually, for an image to be used in a fast-loading Web page, it's important that it's converted to one of the following formats:

- GIF (Graphics Interchange Format).

- JPEG (JPG) (Joint Photographic Experts Group format).

- PNG (Portable Network Graphics format).

These three image formats have been developed especially for onscreen/online use.

What's in a GIF?

You can include graphics other than GIF, JPEG or PNG format in your Web pages by utilising 'Plug-in' technology. However, you do need to ensure your visitors have the correct Plug-in installed on their browsers.

The GIF or Graphics Interchange Format is ideal for simple Web graphics containing a low number of colours such as some logos, icons, buttons, maps and ornate lines. A GIF image is made up of pixels (see the facing page). The colour of each pixel contributes to the colours used in the entire image. The GIF format filters out unnecessary information to provide a compact image file size.

Animated GIFs: used to make up rollover buttons.

The maximum number of colours to use in a Web GIF is 256 – fine for many images but not usually for photos. A series of GIFs can be combined to create a moving image sequence almost like a small movie to create a dynamic or animated-GIF (animation is covered in Chapter 10). A GIF can also have a transparent background, useful if you're using a particular background image in a Web page.

JPEG – the photographic format

Images with greater colour density than simple logos are usually best saved in JPEG format. Given the title, it's no surprise the JPEG (or Joint Photographic Experts Group) file format is ideal for displaying photographic type images on your Web pages:

- JPEG files have the filename extension .jpg.

- Like GIF, JPEG is a high compression format and uses up to about 16.7 million colours.

- However, JPEG files don't convert small text, solid blocks of an image or hard lines as well as GIF.

If you use a scanner to capture images, usually it's best to set the resolution to 100% and scan at 72 dpi. To keep image size small, crop off non-essential parts.

The JPEG image format is perfect for photos, but as with all Web images, try to keep the physical size and file size as low as possible, to help ensure images load quickly on a Web browser

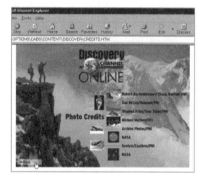

The PNG graphics format

A relatively recent addition to the Web graphics format gallery, PNG or Portable Network Graphics is another high compression format. It's been hailed as the future graphics format ideal for use on the Web. Claims of 30% greater file size compression over the GIF format have been made.

One of PNG's most striking and potentially powerful features is that these images can contain embedded textual information (meta-tags) which can be detected by the Internet search engines. However, it's not all good news. Only some current generation browsers support PNG and different PNG file types exist for both the PC and the Apple Mac. PNG images designed for one platform may not display at their best on the other platform.

Preparing images for the Web

Copyright and legal issues

Images are intellectual property. If the graphics (or any other content) you plan to use are not your own, check with the copyright owner whether you can use them legally in your Web pages. The Web is new legal territory and things may not always be clear. Before using any content that you do not own, get written permission.

Digital watermarking an image

To apply copyright to an image, you can embed a digital watermark into it. DigiMarc is one organisation providing digital watermarking software. Point your browser at: http://www. digimarc.com for more information.

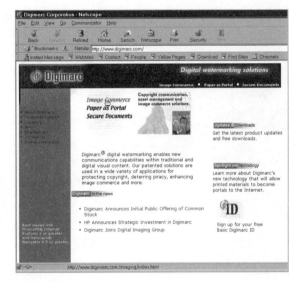

Disabling browser 'Save image...' mouse commands

If you want to apply some direct protection from visitors 'borrowing' images you have created for your site, consider using the (currently free) script available from the Web address below.

The script disables the right mouse button image save commands in Microsoft Internet Explorer v4.x and Netscape Navigator v4.x and all later browsers. It doesn't currently work with Apple Mac PCs and is not a complete solution (the more knowledgeable users may still find your images in their browser cache folders, for example).

http://javascript.internet.com/page-details/no-right-click.html

Optimising images for Web use:

1 To create and prepare your images, use suitable Web graphics editing software like Paint Shop Pro and make sure you choose the Red, Green and Blue (RGB) colour mode.

2 Edit your images at high colour depth (16 million colours) and larger physical sizes.

These images come courtesy of NetObjects Fusion 4 training.

Compare a JPEG image at 256 colours...

... and the same image at 16 million colours

3 When you're ready to place an image on a Web page, make a copy and reduce the physical size of the copy to the size you want, if necessary.

4 Reduce the colour depth of the images to a suitable level: GIF – 256 or 16 colours; JPG – keep to 16 million colours.

5 One of the most important Web image characteristics is the image file size or Kb value. Kb is short for Kilobyte, which is equal to 2^{10} (1024) bytes. In Windows Explorer, with the View > Details command active, you can see the Kb size of any highlighted image. Aim to get this figure as low as possible but without sacrificing image quality.

Interlacing images

Download time for a 40K or more standard GIF image (GIF-87a) can sometimes seem too long. Interlacing allows larger capacity images to appear to be displayed quicker. A visitor can see a low quality definition image (GIF-89a) before it is fully defined.

Interlacing splits an image file into two sets of alternate bands. While the image downloads on a visitor's browser, one set of bands is displayed first – at this point, the entire

When using a logo on a Web page, convert the logo file to GIF format
(unless your logo is particularly complex, in which case consider using JPEG or PNG format instead).
   Compare file sizes and choose the most appropriate.

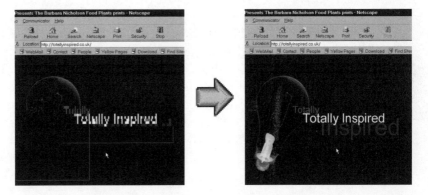

image is visible but indistinct. Only when the other set of bands is fully downloaded is the full image clearly visible. If you want to provide a suspense or surprise element, a non-interlaced GIF-89a format is preferable instead.

Creating an interlaced GIF

You can easily create an interlaced GIF-89a format from a non-interlaced GIF or from many standard image formats using the appropriate commands in any suitable image editing program such as Paint Shop Pro, Adobe Photoshop or GIF Lube.

Progressive JPEG – a similar approach

Ordinary JPEG images can't be interlaced. However, Progressive JPEG – a more recent development of the JPEG standard – provides a similar feature. When a progressive JPEG image downloads, an approximation of the image is displayed on the first cycle with further details added on subsequent cycles until finally the entire image is shown.

Creating transparent images

Sometimes, you may want to place an image on a page, but not want to keep the default image background; you may already have decided to use a specific page background and want that to show through instead giving the impression that the image is transparent. Of the two main image formats examined on previous pages, currently only the GIF-89a format supports image transparency.

How to create a transparent image

The GIF-89a provides additional features over GIF-87a, one of which is image transparency. You can create a transparent GIF-89a by modifying an existing GIF-87a or creating an entirely new image using a suitable application, like Paint Shop Pro. The GIF Construction Set from Alchemy Mindworks is another well known shareware application from which you can create transparent GIFs (also animated or dynamic GIFs as outlined in Chapter 10).

Transparent GIFs help create stunning graphics

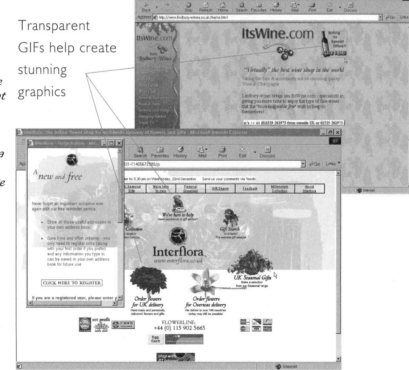

Setting optimal image size

Using pictures and other graphics in Web pages has implications of which you should be aware when considering your page design. One of the most important aspects to consider is the file size of every image or graphic used. By file size, essentially we're referring to the combination of the number of colours used – or colour depth – as well as image physical size. Colour depth is covered overleaf.

The physical size of an image is determined by its horizontal and vertical dimensions. Physical size combined with other factors determines the file size. One benchmark to consider, therefore, is to try and make each image in your Web page use less than about 20- 30 Kb maximum.

While preparing graphics in conversion programs like Paint Shop Pro and Adobe Photoshop, you may be given a choice of palettes. If possible, choose Adaptive or Optimised at the conversion stage if you want to get as close a match as possible to the original image.

Considering download time

The larger the image, the longer it takes to download. Even a small thumbprint image can use many thousands of Kilobytes if not correctly optimised. If a Web page contains multiple images, download time increases correspondingly.

A carefully prepared small image can make a big impact

Establishing ideal colour depth

Colour depth is all about how many colours are used to make up an image. While a GIF image may display adequately using 256 colours, photos usually display poorly at this level (64K or even 16 million colours would probably be best here).

Aim to keep the colour depth as low as possible for the image you're using: ideally 256 colours for GIFs and 32,768 or 65,536 colours for JPEGs. But let the image quality dictate the lowest setting you can use: reduce the colour depth for an image too much and it can appear jagged and patchy. We can also describe colour depth in terms of bits instead of colours. The following table illustrates how colour and bit-depth are related.

The LOWSRC attribute in HTML allows a low resolution image to be downloaded before the main image arrives. A visitor can then decide whether to wait for the main image or to click on another link. However, a compatible browser (like Netscape Navigator/Communicator) is required.

Number of colours:	Is referred to as:
2 colours	1-bit
16 colours	4-bit
256 colours	8-bit
32,768 colours	16-bit
65,536 colours	Also 16-bit
16,777,216 colours	24-bit or 32-bit

16 colours (JPEG)

256 colours (JPEG)

16 million colours (JPEG)

16 colours (GIF)

256 colours (GIF)

16 million colours GIF (unnecessary)

Using thumbnail images

Try to avoid including large photographic-type images in your Web pages. A large photograph could take two or more megabytes of space: this can take quite a while to download, especially when using slower modem connection speeds.

A thumbnail image is a small 'preview' representation of the 'real' full-size image. As a thumbnail image is smaller, it downloads much quicker than the 'main' image and so is an ideal way to reduce download time while still providing the essential content. When a visitor wants to see the main image, they simply click the thumbnail image to open a new window containing the full size image.

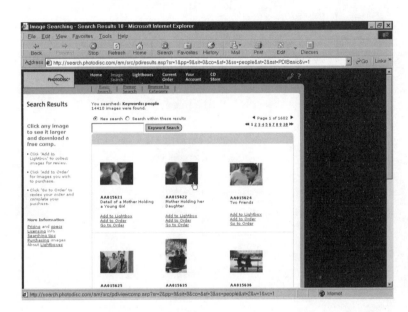

Picture Dicer is a freeware program that can chop a large graphic into smaller sections for speedier downloading and arrange the sections into a neat table.
Point your browser at: www.ziplink.net/ ~shoestring/dicer01.htm

With thumbnails, visitors can choose what to view in detail, rather than having to endure longer download times for irrelevant information. Thumbnail images are ideal when an associated 'main' image is a larger, high resolution, photographic-type image (using the JPEG format).

Thumbnail images demonstrate consideration for your visitors who will most likely have cause to remember such thoughtfulness.

The important point about thumbnail images is that they introduce choice to your visitors. The best advice is to never provide direct access to any large, photographic-type images: try to provide a thumbnail stand-in and let your visitors decide what action they want to take and when.

Providing impact with imagemaps

An imagemap is a single, usually larger than 'normal' image that contains two or more links to other Web pages in the current site or to other Web addresses (URLs).

Each specific area of an imagemap or 'hotspot' is assigned a different link address. A visitor simply clicks the desired hotspot to jump to another Web page or Web address. These defined areas can be irregular in shape or have a more common profile like a button or icon.

Imagemaps can result in larger file sizes than you might expect.
Therefore, this is an area for the Web page designer to watch.

An imagemap is a neat way of including multiple links in a small space. Picture imagemaps are often used as an attractive alternative to a conventional button menu of links.

Always include equivalent text links in an imagemap, to ensure its options are still available even if visitors have turned off graphics display in their browsers.

An imagemap can only be detected by a graphically activated Web browser, not one that is text-based or has graphics detection turned off.

In this example from NetObjects Fusion 4, these areas are defined as hotspots/hyperlinks

You can include an imagemap in a Web page in two ways: client-side or – more rarely nowadays – server-side. Both methods have benefits and drawbacks. However, with a little more work, you can provide the best option by combining both techniques. See your HTML guide for full details.

Creating an imagemap

The better graphical Web design software packages like FrontPage and NetObjects Fusion provide simple commands to create and fine-tune imagemaps or you can use one of the many special applications designed for the job. Your browser search facilities can help you find one.

Including ALT tags

For every image on your Web pages, make sure you include the necessary HTML ALT code to provide a text marker equivalent. Here's why:

- Some visitors may disable the graphics capabilities of their browsers to speed up page download time.

- If a search engine scans your Web site while regularly 'spidering' the Web, by carefully creating text markers for all graphics you can sometimes increase your ranking in a search engine's index.

- Some disabled visitors may not be able to see your graphics and instead rely on text to make sense of a Web page.

Many Internet search engines regularly scan or 'spider' the Web to update their records and find Web sites to include on their indexes. They'll often detect ALT tags if they're available.

Fortunately, you can easily set this up in HTML. Here's an example of the use of the ALT tag:

```
<IMG SRC="ahlogo.gif" HEIGHT=50 WIDTH=200 ALT="Austin Hall logo">
```

You can use single words, phrases and even brief sentences in ALT text descriptions. These can be carefully worded to maximise specific search engine requirements and ranking (Chapter 13). For example, the central text below is a graphic link with 'to Home page' assigned as the ALT label.

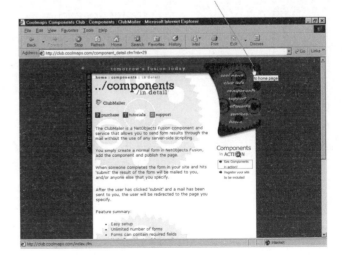

Web graphics round-up: 10 top tips

Like cartoons, line art images (with the addition of a little colour) can translate well onto a Web site. Line art images also compress easily and quickly.

However, perhaps the most value from a Web design aspect is through their simplicity. Often, a simple illustration stands out from the rest.

Don't put larger images at the top of a Home/ Index page. Some visitors may not wait for them to download; if so, you've probably lost them permanently!

1 Don't fall into the common trap of including too many graphics and text in a space. If necessary, break up a page into multiple pages. Then, information is easier to read and pages load faster further enhancing your visitors' experience.

2 On Web pages, images are best measured in pixels. So for Web design, think in terms of pixels (shown in the Step 3 example) rather than centimetres.

3 Use the <WIDTH> and <HEIGHT> HTML tags to help images load in a browser quicker (usually):
<IMG SRC="image.gif" WIDTH=50 HEIGHT=25>

4 For each image or graphic you use, aim to create the smallest graphics file for the best image quality possible.

5 Include a brief text equivalent description using the HTML <ALT> tag for each graphic used.

6 Try to keep photographic-type images to less than 200 pixels horizontally and vertically to reduce time needed to download.

7 To reduce page download time, keep the total graphics content of each page to less than about 50 Kb maximum and reuse the same images wherever possible.

8 Colourful and complex is not always best. Simple line art images, like those found in newspaper cartoons, can sometimes be just as effective as more elaborate images.

9 The Web is essentially a graphical medium so, wherever appropriate, use attractive images on your Web pages. Pictures/graphics are usually better than lots of text – and are usually more interesting from a visitor's viewpoint.

10 Use 'active' empty space to frame your content.

Designing frame-based Web pages

Creating Web pages using frames is like placing several Web pages into a single window. Sounds great doesn't it, but there are pitfalls. Here, you can learn how best to use frames in your Web pages.

Covers

Chapter Eight

Introducing frames

With frames, you can arrange for a desired section of a Web page to stay the same while other parts may change as a visitor navigates through your Web site. Most current browsers can display framed Web sites. However, some early browsers may be unable to display frames.

Arguably, a framed Web site is harder for a search engine spidering program to index. If a higher ranking in the search engine directories is important, consider your framed design carefully to maximise positive results.

On this Microsoft page, 2 frames have been created. The top frame keeps the Microsoft logo and navigation links displayed. The lower frame displays the current page information

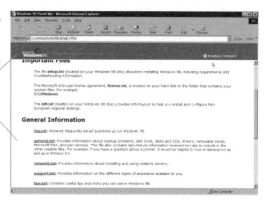

How it all works

A 'normal' HTML Web document uses the <BODY> </BODY> HTML tag-pair. In a framed Web page, the <FRAMESET> </FRAMESET> tag-pair is used in place of the <BODY> tags. Think of a Frameset as a kind of container that holds your framed Web site.

In a framed Web site, the Frameset document needs to download only once to a visitor's browser. As the visitor navigates through the various pages in a site, only the changing content pages need downloading. If you don't want to get too involved with the HTML syntax, most DTP-based Web design software packages provide easy commands to create framed Web sites/pages.

Why multiple frames can be an advertiser's best friend

In Web pages that are essentially advertising-driven, frames can be particularly valuable. Using a framed approach, you can set up your design so that a banner, advertising slogan, or compelling animation is held in place while a visitor navigates in the adjacent frames.

Frame types

You can use a variety of frame options in your Web pages:

- **Basic frames** – Set up areas of the screen with standard borders by default (usually available in all browsers that support frames). A variety of attributes, colours and shades can also be applied.

- **Multiple frames** – several frames are possible.

- **Floating frames** – currently another Microsoft Internet Explorer feature which provides frames which can be sited anywhere in the browser window.

- **Linking frames** – enables a visitor to click on a hyperlink in one frame (say one of a list of buttons) to cause the content of another linked frame to change (the target of the clicked button).

- **Borderless frames** – available with later versions of Netscape Navigator/Communicator and Microsoft's Internet Explorer. Can help produce snappy results.

- **Frames containing custom borders** – again, this is a Microsoft Internet Explorer enhancement to-date, and allows you to specify background colours.

Don't design a framed Web site that forces a visitor to scroll from left to right to read the page content. This usually irritates visitors; some simply won't put up with it and move to another easier site.

In HTML you can establish frame sizes using the number of rows, columns, percentages or pixels.

Example HTML for a 2-frame Web page:

1 The Top frame, fixed.

2 The lower frame. Scrollbars appear when necessary.

```
Readme - Notepad
File  Edit  Search  Help
<!DOCTYPE HTML PUBLIC "-//W3C//DTD HTML 3.2 Final//EN">
<html>
<!DOCTYPE HTML PUBLIC "-//W3C//DTD HTML 3.2 Final//EN">

<head>
<title>Windows 98 Read Me</title>
</head>

<frameset framespacing="2" frameborder="no" rows="65,*">
  <frame src="readm_01.htz" name="top" margintop="0" scrolling="no"
noresize>
  <frame src="readm_02.htz" name="MAIN_FRAME" scrolling="auto">
  <noframes>
  <body bgcolor="#FFFFFF">
  <p>This web page uses frames, but your browser doesn't support them.</p>
  </body>
  </noframes>
</frameset>

<frameset>
  <noframes>
  </noframes>
</frameset>
</html>
```

Using frames in a Web page

A separate frame can sometimes provide an ideal container for a rotating banner advert or animated Java-type news component.

Deciding whether to use frames is often not as simple as it may first appear and so needs careful consideration. For some applications, frames can save huge amounts of time. But some users simply don't like them. Let's take a closer look and examine some of the benefits and drawbacks:

Benefits:

- Each frame can be considered to be a separate window and as such can contain a completely separate HTML document.

- A 'fixed' frame is an ideal container into which you can place items that normally would not change from page to page, like a logo, marketing message, toolbar or standard button links.

- Frames can help provide a kind of grand tour of a range of products, Web site, building, and so on.

- Frame links can be tied together so that carrying out an action in one frame can cause changes to occur in another frame. Some spectacular effects can be achieved using this technique.

- A frame can include a border that is displayed or hidden. Multiple frames with hidden borders, with each frame containing its own active content, can be compelling and spectacular.

Drawbacks:

- Frames usually take longer to download; you need to be sure this will be tolerated by your visitors.

- Having several active frames makes things more hectic and may confuse visitors or blur the main message of the page.

- Framed Web sites usually make search engine spidering programs work harder, to say the least.

- Not all browsers can deal with frames. Ideally, you may also have to include an equivalent 'frameless' version for those visitors who require it.

Hands-on Action guidelines

Consider the following guidelines for deciding whether to use frames and, if so, ensuring you have a trouble-free frame experience:

1 Too many frames can cause confusion and lengthen download times. Keep to no more than 3 frames, unless you have a convincing reason to include a fourth.

Test your new framed Web page designs using several different Web browsers to ensure they work properly.

2 Working with frames in HTML is harder than working with non-framed pages. Frames can be troublesome. Poor frame designs can be a nightmare!

3 Some older browsers can't understand frames. Visitors with these browsers may feel alienated unless you provide non-framed pages also. However, this dual approach can double your workload and significantly increase the amount of time spent maintaining and updating your pages.

A browser's Back button may not work properly when viewing a framed Web site.

4 With frames, it's easy to end up making too much information available to a visitor at one time, causing confusion and conflict between different elements. Your central message may then be missed by your visitors.

5 Place the HTML <NOFRAMES> and </NOFRAMES> tag-pair into the Frameset document to enter information, search engine key words and meta tags that only frame-incompatible browsers will see. Careful choices here can help improve your site's ranking in some search engines.

6 If possible, include a component that tests whether a visitor is using a frame-enabled browser and, if not, arrange for a statement to be displayed on the screen stating that fact: *'This site/page uses frames but your browser either doesn't support them or has frames turned off'.*

Helping visitors break out of frames

If you're not using frames in your Web design, sometimes a visitor may log onto your site still trapped in a frame from a previous framed Web site.

The drawback from this condition is that they will see the Web address or URL of the previously visited Web site in their browser's Location/Address box while viewing and navigating your Web site.

Don't use this 'breakout' script if you're using frames in your own Web pages.

This is one result you probably don't want – especially if you're in business. You can just never know: the previous Web site could be your main competitor, ouch!

So what can you do? Fear not, here's some simple JavaScript code that you can enter into your Web page to help your visitor break free and return their browser to it's normal condition:

1 Insert the following code as high as possible between the <HEAD> and </HEAD> tags in your HTML so that the script will run before your page has fully downloaded.

2 Text
```
<SCRIPT LANGUAGE="JavaScript">
<!— Start
if (parent.location.href != window.location.href)
parent.location.href = window.location.href
// — End —>
</SCRIPT>
```

If you're serious about creating some neat special effects in your Web pages, deciding to take some time to learn the basics of JavaScript is always a worthwhile investment. You can learn more about JavaScript – and have some fun – from the companion book in this series: 'JavaScript in easy steps'.

Including audio in your Web site

The ability to include background sounds, voices and music adds a whole new dimension to a Web page. This chapter explains the basics, shows how to include sound components and explores the latest techniques.

Covers

Chapter Nine

The basics of audio on the Web

Sound offers the Web page designer exciting possibilities. It can enliven a Web page and may be especially valuable for visitors with vision problems. Sometimes, a simple piece of music can single-handedly create in your visitor the mood you want to achieve. Also, unlike pictures that may need supporting text to make sense, sound content can stand on its own without any further support needed.

Powerful reasons why sound can benefit a site

While perhaps viewing a page, a visitor could listen to a voice accompaniment. Here are two powerful benefits from including simple voice recordings:

- Background or support information.

- Help or assistance for visitors.

Web sound components come in two flavours: digital or synthesized audio format. Often, providers of the various sound technologies make available free plug-ins for their particular sound technology. So what else is possible?

- Discrete sound clips – the relevant file must be fully downloaded before the component can play.

- Live audio streaming – a visitor can listen to the sound while the relevant file downloads.

- Live audio, talk shows, news, etc. – a visitor can hear what is being delivered as it actually happens.

What a visitor needs to hear Web sounds

Two conditions must be met before Web sounds can be heard by visitors:

1. Their PC must contain the necessary sound hardware, either a sound card or sound chips installed directly onto the motherboard (plus speakers). Most PCs/ Apple Macs now include sound support.

2. Their default browser must support the appropriate sound format being used or have the correct plug-in or helper application correctly installed and set up.

Popular sound formats

Microsoft Windows comes with the Sound Recorder utility. You can use Sound Recorder to record, play and edit any WAVe files you want to include in your Web pages.

For more information, see your Windows documentation.

Before you can use a background sound component for a Web page, the sound clip must first be converted into an appropriate format. Currently, several popular formats exist, including for example:

- WAVe format (.wav) – can play on both the Microsoft Windows and Apple Mac platforms. Visitors using Macs with Netscape browsers need Netscape Navigator v3.0 or later.

- MIDI (.midi, .mid) Musical Instrument Digital Interface – another popular format often used to tie in with musical instruments and synthesizers. MIDI files are compatible with most operating systems.

- AIFF (.aiff) Audio Interchange File Format – originally designed for the Apple Mac. Can now play on Windows 9x and later PCs with the correct plug-in.

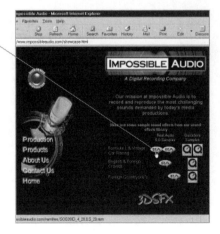

Some of the latest presentation software packages include plug-ins which can enable a Web page provider to broadcast a presentation on the Web. To gain further information, check out the latest versions of Lotus Freelance Graphics and Microsoft PowerPoint.

- AU (.au) format: often used in Java applets, NeXT systems and Sun Microsystems PCs.

- MPEG (.mpg) – Motion Pictures Expert Group format. Is also used for video files.

- RealAudio (.ra, .ram) – a popular current choice, plays streaming (live continuous play) audio. Your Web host will need the correct RealAudio server software installed. Visitors need the RA Player browser plug-in.

- Rich Music Format (.rmf) – may be lesser known than previous examples. Can be used in interactive environments like the Web.

Exploring musical possibilities

Music can affect people in a variety of ways. If you want to put over a particular mood in a Web site, musical content can help considerably. Consider the basics:

- Fast, dynamic music emphasizes action, tension or excitement.

- Contrastingly of course, slow and lingering music can help evoke a feeling of calmness and relaxation.

- Also, the right kind of music for a Web site doesn't need any further explanation: music is its own language.

If you're trying to create a particular mood, I suggest that the musical content of a Web page usually works best if it contains characteristics that make it soothing and calming, rather than exciting or stirring.

Longer musical sequences can put a greater strain on visitors' computer resources, whilst shorter bursts are less open to error and can sometimes be just as effective.

Let's explore some ideas of the kinds of Web sites that might benefit from including music components:

- An English gardening site could include a few opening bars of an English dawn chorus carefully recorded at daybreak in Spring.

- A geographical Web site with an Australian interest could include a short sequence of an Aboriginal didgeridoo to evoke the mood of the outback.

- A corporate site could include a few confident, powerful and stimulating bars – just as the Home/Index page loads and the corporate logo emerges.

- Imagine a travel-based Web site is running a special holiday promotion to say, Mexico. A few bars of traditional Mexican music can really set the scene as photos of Mexican culture and scenery are teased into view with the latest incredible travel offers temptingly woven into the presentation.

This way of thinking can be applied to any Web site theme and can enhance your presentation, leaving a memorable impression with your visitor. A perfect reason to revisit!

Installing sound on a Web page

Both music and voice accompaniments can be arranged to play when a Web page displays or when a visitor clicks a specific button or moves their mouse across a designated location on the screen.

'Humanising' the Web

One of the most powerful aspects of voice recordings is the human element. Although the Web is a powerful medium, it has still an essentially electronic, distant 'feel' to it. Contrastingly, the tonal highs and lows of a voice recording can put over personality and individuality.

Sound files can have copyright applied to them. If you use other people's material, get written permission first and always keep a copy in your records.

However, visitors can become irritated if a recording plays for too long. Therefore, try to aim for the minimum time possible; have a specific purpose in mind and try to avoid cramming too much into the sound sequence.

Sound components installation

Using the correct HTML, you can embed sound components into a Web page or link them to it. Embedded sound components are usually downloaded automatically when a visitor logs on to a Web page. Linked sound components usually include control buttons to enable visitors to decide if they want to play the sequence.

Here's a great idea for a personal Web page containing a CV that can really help you to get noticed. Amaze and impress prospective employers by including a carefully crafted optional RealAudio sound file with a Start/Stop button.

WAVe files can be created easily using the Windows Sound Recorder utility. You can also create files in other formats using one of the many dedicated sound recorder applications available.

For visitors using Microsoft Internet Explorer browsers, sound files installed using the HTML <BGSOUND> tag can be set to play a specific number of times, or continuously whilst the page containing the sounds remains displayed.

However, to cover most browsers, usually, the HTML <EMBED> tag is a better choice as it is supported in most current browsers including Netscape v2.0 and later versions.

See your HTML guide or Web design software documentation for more precise information.

RealAudio: live audio streaming

In a Web page containing a discrete sound clip, the sound file has to fully download to a visitor's browser before it can play. With live audio streaming, however, sound can be played/heard while downloading to a visitor's browser.

You can discover more about RealAudio technology at Progressive Networks' Web site. Point your browser at: www.realaudio .com/

RealAudio from Progressive Networks is currently one of the most popular live audio streaming systems on the Net. However, a visitor's browser must support live audio streaming – some older browsers may not.

Also, your Web host must support the variety of RealAudio technology you want to use, so liaise closely with them to determine the options available to you.

The RealPlayer playing a sound clip

Many radio stations worldwide now use RealAudio technology to deliver their programmes to the world through the Web.

Creating RealAudio content

You'll need to download and install the following (currently free) software: 1. RealProducer G2 and 2. RealProducer Authoring Kit. Try: http://

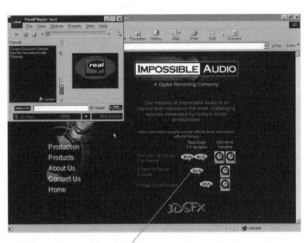

Here, each RealAudio sound clip is accessible using the buttons

www.realnetworks.com/developers/index.html

Next, you can learn how to create RealAudio using the superb guides available from real.com. Try: http://service.real.com/help/library/guides/production/realpgd.htm

1 This Web site provides RealMedia for visitors with 'slow' modems, and...

To provide a RealAudio-based news service, simply follow the guidelines listed in the RealAudio section earlier in this chapter.

2 ... a 'FAST MODEM/ ISDN' option for visitors who have faster links to the Internet.

Delivering a news service

Audio news providers often broadcast directly onto the Web using RealAudio technology. Some news organisations also provide a text-based equivalent of their audio content for those visitors who want to keep viewing more private. Providing a Web news service stretches the resources of the Web and can create new problems, the most important of which concerns maintenance and upkeep. News, by its nature, happens all the time and events can change fast, creating huge logistical problems for site providers.

For Web-based news sites to succeed, the content has to be compelling, relevant and interesting enough for visitors to want to return again and again to the site.

You can add free newsfeeds to your site from www.moreover.com/

Here are just four examples of the kind of Web sites that could benefit from providing a Web-based news service:

- Organisations can include speeches and interviews made by key industry movers and shakers.

- Travel-oriented Web sites could include news about travel conditions in key parts of the world.

- Web sites covering sports events like the round the world yacht races could include up-to-date news reports about the latest developments.

- Fashion-based Web pages could include talks from famous designers and models about the latest trends to hit their industry. And so on.

Web audio top tips

1 Consider carefully whether you really need audio. Sound demands more from a visitor's PC, requires sound hardware, and maybe a special plug-in at the browser end.

2 If you decide to include a sound component in your Web site, consider carefully whether you should set this to autoplay as soon as a visitor arrives at your page. Some visitors may become irritated with your choice of music.

3 For a site containing autoplay music, consider including a Stop/Mute button and let your visitors choose.

4 Currently, the <BGSOUND> tag works only in those browsers that support it, like Internet Explorer, but not Netscape browsers. Netscape browsers make extensive use of plug-ins to handle a range of different file types.

5 Avoid using sound content to duplicate what is already included in your text. Provide essential information in text form and let audio content complement your presentation. Consider including a brief text description/overview of each audio component included.

6 Try to avoid including single sentence sound extracts: visitors may expect more and so become puzzled or irritated.

7 The simpler conventional sound formats .wav and .mid are ideal for sound clips of up to about 1 minute's duration. Any longer than this and visitors may become impatient.

8 Audioconferencing technology can also provide an ideal environment in which to informally discuss a range of issues, following in the Internet café and virtual clubs tradition.

Animating your Web pages

Movement, animation, sound and video components can all provide impact and grab the attention of your visitors. But success here needs careful consideration and handling. This chapter explores what is possible.

Covers

Chapter Ten

Introducing Web animation

Gaining animation skills

To apply complex animation-type components in your Web pages successfully requires some extra knowledge and skills using a variety of multimedia-type authoring programs, some of which may be expensive. As with any complex software, the process takes time and effort.

Under the guidance of a skilled graphic designer, incredibly effective results can be achieved with tools from Macromedia (for example). However, expensive and powerful software cannot make up for poor design choices.

There's nothing stopping anyone from obtaining the necessary tools and learning these skills. Just allow for the extra time you think you'll need, then double it!

Therefore, if your Web project is particularly urgent, it may be more cost-effective simply to 'buy in' the necessary skills from appropriate contract programmers and graphic artists rather than have to repeat the exercise several times later.

Understanding more about your visitors

Visitors can be considered as readers or viewers (or a little of both).

Viewers don't necessarily like to read a lot of information onscreen; they may prefer visual impact. They seek a seductive experience and journey – not the destination. A tantalising wash of colour, fun and variety wrapped up in a few emotive words and phrases. Viewers usually love animation in all its forms.

Readers however, are different; they have a clear goal; they're seeking something specific in your Web site. Often, they may turn off graphics capabilities in their browsers to speed up access to the information they want.

To design your site for readers, pack it with lots of relevant information and make it load fast over almost any Web browser and Internet connection; and provide easy to use, alternative ways to access the same information.

Applying flashing components

If you want to attract a visitor's attention quickly, a flashing object certainly gets noticed. However, consider this route carefully. Usually, the central purpose of a Web site is its message. A flashing component can also draw a visitor's attention away from the main message and too many conflicting elements can cause visitor confusion. Consider:

- Anything flashing on a Web page exerts a powerful pull on a visitor's attention.

- Including multiple flashing objects on a Web page can create its own special brand of chaos, or provide stimulating excitement: the key point here is to carefully establish what is appropriate.

Paragraphs are usually best left as plain text: a visitor needs time to focus on your message. Anything that interferes with this essential process doesn't usually help.

Flashing logos

A flashing logo may appear too 'loud' or inappropriate for an organisation. Furthermore, the nature of a logo and therefore the branding changes, possibly resulting in serious damage to the image of an organisation. Therefore, consider the idea carefully before implementing this action in a corporate-type Web page. Nevertheless, a flashing logo in a lighter context may work well when considered carefully as part of the whole presentation.

Flashing text

A quick way to steal a visitor's attention: provide a single headline or short sentence, suggest impact or urgency, and arrange for it to blink. Like a lighthouse beacon, flashing text exerts a powerful pull on the eye. Likewise, a flashing frame tends to draw the eye towards the frame contents. If this is what you're aiming for, fine (remember, some earlier browsers may not be able to handle frames properly).

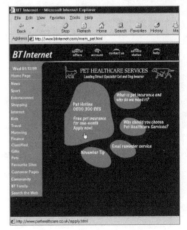

A flashing special offer message can really get noticed!

Using animated GIFs

Static Web pages don't include any movement or animation, only text and ideally some graphics content. Dynamic Web pages include components which provide action or movement of some kind. Although the idea of dynamic Web pages may at first seem more appealing, it's possible for this aspect to be overdone.

Animated Web pages demand more from a browser than their static counterparts. For example, using too many dynamic GIFs with infinite loops can use up an excessive amount of a visitor's computer resources and so create temporary operating system instability.

Sometimes, a static Web page can be adequate for your needs and it can put over the desired impression simply but effectively. However, if you feel your Web page is missing that 'extra something', one answer might be to 'spice up' the page by adding an animated or dynamic GIF.

What's a dynamic GIF?

A dynamic GIF is simply several slightly different GIF images linked together to form a chain almost like a film sequence. For example, there may be ten or fifteen frames in such a sequence.

Ideally, a dynamic GIF should be carefully designed to produce a small physical size. However, remember that a poorly designed and badly prepared dynamic GIF is arguably worse than using a single still image.

A dynamic GIF can be set up to:

Be careful not to provide too much movement on a page to avoid creating a condition whereby a visitor's eye is continually attracted to various, sometimes opposing, elements thus creating confusion. A visitor can then miss any central message entirely!

- Run through its sequence once when a visitor logs on to a Web page.

- Loop through a sequence a set number of times. The interval between each frame can also be specified.

- Loop indefinitely (see the tips).

Creating a dynamic GIF

A wide range of applications are now available to help you create dynamic or animated GIFs. You can use standalone programs like Animation Shop from PaintShop Pro, and software like GIF Animator from Alchemy MindWorks at: www.mindworkshop.com/ Or you can learn to use the animation tools that may come built in as part of the top quality Web design software products.

Microsoft's ActiveX

In some ways a complement to Java, Microsoft's ActiveX enables a specific applet to be designed to perform a specific task. ActiveX applications include: multimedia animation, virtual reality, calendars, animated buttons, Web forms, viewing Microsoft Office files in Internet Explorer, video sequences and other types of dynamic Web content. Quite a few Web sites, like the example below, make ActiveX Components available for download free of charge.

If a browser needs an ActiveX control that is not present, usually the control is downloaded automatically from an appropriate site on the Web.

To discover more about ActiveX, point your browser at: http:// www.activex.com/

Shockwave (page 99) was one of the first ActiveX controls to be included with Microsoft's Internet Explorer and Windows 9x. Other ActiveX controls include RealAudio as discussed in Chapter 9.

ActiveX components run on any PC that has an ActiveX-compliant Web browser installed – like for example, Microsoft's Internet Explorer from v3.0.

Like Java, you can create your own ActiveX controls, or you can find many already available on the Web (see the tips).

Including ActiveX components in your Web pages

To place an ActiveX component in your Web page, you can use the HTML <OBJECT> tag or use the appropriate commands in your Web design software. See your documentation for the exact syntax you need.

Java and Java Beans

Working with Java (from Sun Microsystems)

Java is a programming language that you can use to create multimedia Web components. A Java applet is a small type of Java program that can be placed on a HTML Web page.

Java applets usually work best on Pentium-grade computers to benefit fully from the special effects they provide.

Examples include sophisticated animation sequences, often including sound and video clips and the now familiar ticker-tape streamers that provide up-to-date relevant news often visible on many Web pages. Java applets are also platform-independent so can run on Microsoft Windows, Apple Macs and UNIX operating systems without any need for further editing or modification!

A Java applet must download to a visitor's PC completely before it can run. Contrast this trait with JavaScript on the next page.

Java demands more of a PC's resources and slows down page loading. The viewing browser must also support Java. Some PCs may not be able to handle Java properly possibly leading to confusion and poor presentation on those PCs.

Providing Java applets in your Web pages

Consider the following guidelines:

*   You can learn to write your own applets. Java is a continually developing language.

*   Lots of different applets have already been developed (see the tips). Simply modify these to work correctly.

There are lots of sites on the Web from which you can download free Java applets. Use the search engines and directories to find the ones you want.

To place a Java applet on a Web page, use the <APPLET> tag and its attributes as described in your HTML guide or Web design software. You'll need .class files and several other types of files to install an applet.

Using Java Beans in a Web page

A Java Bean is a Java applet designed to be one component in a larger application; unlike a Java applet which requires several type of files, a Java Bean contains all you need to install the applet.

Example Beans are sometimes provided with Web design applications that support them. For example, NetObjects Fusion v4.0 includes an example Bean that calculates the current date and time in several geographical locations.

JavaScript and JScript

Developed by Netscape, JavaScript is a type of programming language loosely related to Java; JavaScript is considered to be less complex and so easier to learn. However, like Java, JavaScript has the potential to cause security problems – sometimes linked to computer viruses.

A JavaScript component can run as soon as a Web page loads or can be activated by a visitor clicking on a button or other trigger point on a Web page.

A cookie lets you store some brief basic information on a visitor's PC for use later when the visitor re-visits the relevant cookie-driven Web site.

JavaScript is often used to place cookies (see the first tip) in a Web page, to help record key information such as a visitor's browser, plug-ins, operating system and display monitor resolution. When a visitor next logs on to a Web site, a cookie can help identify that visitor so that a personalised 'Welcome back' message is displayed.

Including JavaScript in a Web page

A JavaScript applet does not have to be downloaded fully to work, and is therefore usually faster than pure Java.

As with Java, you can learn JavaScript and write your own JavaScript components. Alternatively, you can download predesigned components and modify these to work with your Web pages. Whichever option you choose, it's useful to learn at least the basics of JavaScript (see the details for 'JavaScript in easy steps' on the inside rear cover).

You can insert JavaScript using the <SCRIPT> tag in HTML or by arranging for the JavaScript code to run when a specified event occurs. See your Web design software, HTML and JavaScript guides for detailed design options.

JScript

JScript represents Microsoft's alternative to JavaScript. Whereas JavaScript was developed with Netscape Navigator in mind, JScript is tightly integrated with the Microsoft Internet Explorer series of Web browsers. Unfortunately, this often means that a component developed for JScript may not work under JavaScript.

However, with some knowledge of language variations, it's possible to write a script that works correctly in both Internet Explorer and Netscape Navigator, for example.

Example JavaScript: detecting a visitor's Web browser

Here's an example of how JavaScript can be used to detect whether a visitor is using Microsoft Internet Explorer 4.x or later. If yes, in this example the visitor is redirected to an alternative Index page on the server of the imaginary site 'Yourcompany' containing the more powerful DHTML animated effects.

When entering JavaScript code, you must use straight quotes (" and ') not curly quotes.

The script below could be placed between the <HEAD> and </HEAD> tags in the default Home/Index page.

```
<SCRIPT>
<!—
if ((navigator.userAgent.indexOf("MSIE")!=-1) && navigator.app
Version.substring(0,1) > 3)
{
window.location.replace("http://www.Yourcompany.com/
index_mie4.html");
}
//—>
</SCRIPT>
```

While viewing Java-based Web pages, you can usually view the source code by choosing the appropriate browser command while the page is displayed. For example, in Microsoft Internet Explorer simply open the View menu and choose the Source command.

Modify the script above substituting the Web address and Index page name you want. The main drawback with this approach is the increased development time required.

This site is a superb source if you want to learn more about JavaScript

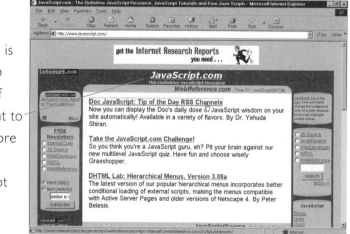

Using rollover buttons and pictures

Rollover is a term used to describe a picture, icon or button that changes when the mouse pointer is moved over it. Other names that refer to rollovers include: mousover, hover and animated (buttons). The currently popular rollover technique usually involves JavaScript code and provides another useful tool in the Web designer's toolkit. As a result, rollovers are simple to write, use little code and so therefore run quickly in a Web browser.

Because rollovers are appealing, it's easy to fall into the trap of providing rollover components that do little to add to the value of a page. Yet, with careful design, rollovers can provide an attractive, effective addition to a Web page.

Rollovers won't work with imagemap-type graphics. Imagemaps have hotspots defined as hyperlinks instead.

How rollovers work

A rollover image is actually two images: one image that forms the default or 'Off' condition and one to create the 'On' condition. For the rollover to be seamless, both images must be the same size and shape. As the images must display quickly, often small GIF image formats are used (see Chapter 7 for more information about images).

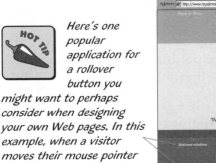

Here's one popular application for a rollover button you might want to perhaps consider when designing your own Web pages. In this example, when a visitor moves their mouse pointer onto the button, the rollover displays more details about that particular section.

Popular uses for rollovers

Rollovers can be particularly effective when used as part of image text buttons. For example, a dark blue hyperlinked Web navigation button could, when the mouse pointer is placed on it, change to, say, a lighter blue or soft grey. Move the mouse pointer away and the original dark blue returns.

A tiny percentage of Web browsers still don't support JavaScript. Visitors using these browsers may not be able to see any rollovers you create.

Or, imagine you have a Web shop. For each product, you have a small thumbnail image. You can design a rollover so that when a visitor places the mouse pointer onto the image, the product picture is replaced with its current price, until our imaginary visitor moves the mouse pointer away to reveal the original thumbnail image.

ShopFactory™
e-commerce

This approach allows pieces of crucial information to occupy the same physical space and provides the price only to those visitors who wish to know it, contributing to a more 'clean' design structure and enabling more empty (but active) space to be utilised.

When preparing images for use in rollovers, make sure that none of your GIF images are transparent. A transparent image will show the other image that makes up the rollover pair.

Creating a rollover

Many of the current Web design and graphics software packages like NetObjects Fusion, Microsoft FrontPage and Macromedia Fireworks provide commands to create rollovers.

However, below is a basic example rollover HTML code:

```
<A HREF="rollover12.html"
onMouseover="document.but.src='images/button12_on.gif';"
onMouseout="document.but.src='images/button12_off.gif';">
<IMG SRC="images/button12_off.gif" NAME="but"
ALT="[Product/Price rollover button]"></A>
```

Whatever label you use in 'NAME=... ' above, (We've used the label 'but' in our example) remember, you must also place the label between 'document' and 'src' as shown.

Animating text on a Web page

Grabbing attention with JavaScript text boxes

JavaScript can be used to create a small text box window (with a vertical scroll bar if necessary) that can contain cycling testimonials. Imagine the powerful value of 7 or 8 brief cycling testimonials each with say an onscreen display time of about 5 seconds. For businesses especially, real, verifiable testimonials have immense selling power.

You can create text boxes like this using simple JavaScript commands. Or with NetObjects Fusion, you can purchase Components from companies like www.coolmaps.com/ Using the Coolmaps' 'RoboText' Component, you don't need to know JavaScript, just follow the 2-step simple instructions and the job is done. Currently, you can see an example of this superb technique on the Ask Jeeves Home page (www.askjeeves.com/).

Animating the browser status bar

Using JavaScript, you can arrange for a visitor's browser status bar to show scrolling messages. From a marketing aspect, this can be an excellent idea to include up-to-the-minute information or details of special offers, etc.

Scrolling messages are nice and do not interfere with the rest of the display!

The downside is that this effect can usually cause a Web page to load more slowly in your visitor's browser. If your page loads quickly, this may not be a problem, but for graphically-rich Web pages, it's best avoided.

Adding a ticker-tape streamer

An ideal way to quickly help focus a visitor's attention is to provide a line of text scrolling across the screen; this scrolling marquee is much like a ticker-tape streamer. Ticker-tape banners can provide an eye-catching headline to communicate something important, announce a special promotion or to evoke tension.

There are several ways you can do this in a Web page, for example, using:

- the HTML <MARQUEE> </MARQUEE> tag-pair.

- the Java language.

- JavaScript.

Note: currently, the HTML <MARQUEE> tag is supported by Internet Explorer but not Netscape browsers. Browsers that support this feature will then scroll text across the screen as defined by the HTML/Java/JavaScript parameters.

Creating ticker tape streamers is easy with modern Web design software like Microsoft FrontPage and NetObjects Fusion. Using the TickerTape2 Component from www.coolmaps.com for NetObjects Fusion, you can also specify font, colours and the type of text movement.

Here's one ideal application for a ticker tape streamer. This Web site wants to draw particular attention to their range of alternative payment options. So as soon as the Home page loads, the animated movement draws the eye in to the initial focus point: the ticker tape streamer.

Captivating with Shockwave

With Macromedia Shockwave, you can create high quality multimedia, animated graphics and sound components that download quickly in a browser. Shockwave is powerful: text, graphics, animation, video and sound sequences can all be combined easily. Efficient compression ensures these highly animated sequences can be downloaded relatively quickly.

 A Plug-in is a mini program attached to your browser and which allows your browser to handle unusual file formats.

 For a browser to read Shockwave, it must have the appropriate Shockwave Plug-in installed and set up.

The latest versions of Netscape Navigator/ Communicator and Microsoft's Internet Explorer are, by default, set up to handle basic Shockwave files.

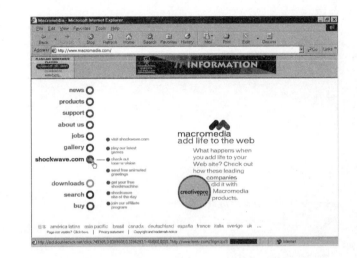

Shockwave animations usually work best when supporting the main theme made up of simple text and graphics. Web pages containing Shockwave and ActiveX content demand more resources from a PC than those containing more traditional Web page elements. A visitor to a Web page containing these components will benefit fully when using a PC equipped with a CPU of 75 MHz or faster.

As Shockwave is a bitmap-based format, components take longer to download compared to components made using newer vector technologies like Flash (see overleaf). Shockwave files use the .dir and .dcr file formats and come in several varieties that are usually updated regularly.

You can include Shockwave technology (or any other Plug-in) on a Web page using the <EMBED> tag on your HTML document. The best Web design applications provide easy-to-use commands to place your ActiveX components on the page. See your Web design software guide for more details.

Entertaining with Flash

Flash essentially now sets the standard if you want to create high quality interactive and animated Web components. Flash enables a designer to create Flash 'movies' that are scalable and use vector technology (rather than bitmap).

For more information about Flash technology, see: http://www.macromedia .com/software/flash/

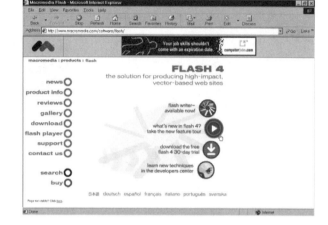

If you plan to include animated components in your Web pages, the Internet search engines are ideal tools to help you find out as much as possible about the subject you want.

Essentially, this means Flash files (.swf format) are small, usually download more quickly than the earlier Shockwave technology and so provide fast playback on typical modem-based connections.

To 'play' Flash animations, the Flash Player is required at the browser end. The good news is that the Flash Player is now provided as part of the Windows 98 and Apple Mac operating systems.

Typically, a Flash file uses an area called 'the stage' in which to arrange several 'frames' that make up the movie sequence. A skilled Flash designer can create interesting, attractive and compelling animations that load quickly in a Flash-enabled Web browser.

Using a later version of Flash you can even arrange for a static image to be seen for those browsers that don't have the Flash Player installed! Typical uses include Web advert banners and unique user interfaces. If a Flash animation does not appear to work properly, ask you Web host to check that they have the correct MIMIE types installed for Flash.

Introducing Web video technology

Web video enables film, TV and news clips to be made available through a Web page in two different ways:

For live video streaming to work, a visitor's browser must support this feature, either naturally or by having the appropriate plug-in installed.

- A discrete video clip file that must be fully downloaded before it can be viewed (early systems).

- A live video streaming clip which can be viewed as it is downloading (latest technology).

If a browser does not have the correct RealMedia plug-in installed, usually it is automatically downloaded.

Benefits

- Video is humanising: it can put over warmth, personality, emotion, feelings, tension and passion.

- International visitors may understand spoken language better than text on your Web pages.

- Moving pictures can describe complexities effectively.

- Video is undoubtedly a powerful advertising medium!

Drawbacks

A 'bad' video can actually damage credibility. Consider your Web video strategy carefully.

- Web video can make heavy demands on a visitor's PC.

- The technology is still a relatively new and complex development requiring more complex tools.

- Spoken language may be difficult to understand.

Evaluating whether Web video is for you

Consider the following guidelines:

1. Read all of the pages relating to the use of video in this chapter. Use the Web to find out more information.

2. Few visitors will wait more than 3 or 4 minutes maximum for a file to download, unless the benefit is clear. Try to keep files sizes small to minimise downloading time.

3. For visitors with slower modem connections, downloading video files may be impractical. Assess your visitors' needs.

4. To put over a mood of fast action, changing scenes or subtle movement, video may be ideal. If you want to encourage pause and consideration, it's usually best to stick with carefully crafted text and graphics content.

5. Always remember: ill-considered use of video can overshadow the central message – usually best left as text.

For more information about QuickTime, point your browser at: www.apple.com/ quicktime/

If the video sequence you want to use is brief, consider using Shockwave or Flash: their file sizes are smaller than conventional video and so usually download quicker.

Apple's QuickTime Player: http://www.apple.com/quicktime/

Popular Web video technologies

Microsoft AVI file format (.avi)

AVI (Audio Video Interleaved) remains one of the most popular multimedia formats for adding discrete movie content to a Web site.

If movement is an important feature of your Web site, a video sequence can arguably illustrate what you want to put over better than any other type of content.

QuickTime Multimedia (.mov, .qt)

QuickTime is a popular multimedia software system from Apple. In a QuickTime 'movie', you can include graphics, text, music, video, sound and 3D components. However, for visitors to view a QuickTime clip in your Web page, they must have the correct QuickTime plug-in installed for their browser and operating system.

MPEG movies (.mpg, .mpeg, .mpe, .mpv)

Web browser plug-ins necessary to view MPEG files are available for Microsoft Windows and the Apple Macintosh.

The Vivo Active Producer format (.viv)

The Vivo multimedia format is supported by Microsoft Windows and the Apple Mac and also requires an appropriate browser plug-in/player to view the movie files.

A fast ISDN or ADSL Internet connection provides an ideal environment in which to view RealVideo files. Although ISDN/ADSL is still comparatively expensive, prices are expected to fall substantially.

RealMedia (.rm, .ra) and RealPlayer Media (.rpm)

With live video streaming, visitors can play and view a video clip *while* it's downloading so they do not have to download a large file just to identify what it's about. One of the most popular live video streaming technologies is RealVideo from Progressive Networks. RealVideo offers significant advantages over previous delivery systems:

- RealVideo player software installed on a visitor's PC can sense when there's heavy Internet traffic and compensate to minimise problems. RealVideo aims to provide the most stable picture quality possible under varying conditions.

- Additional controls like Fast Forward, Rewind and Search are easier to integrate with RealVideo streaming technology.

- RealVideo also includes advanced error correction.

Including video on a Web page

A video component can be embedded into a Web page or linked to it. An embedded video clip is usually downloaded automatically when a visitor logs on to the Web page. A linked component usually includes control buttons to enable visitors to decide if they want to play the sequence. To include a video in a Web page, perform the following:

The latest Web browsers come with video players built in. For example. Netscape includes LiveVideo. Consider including a link to the source site so visitors can easily gain access to the appropriate plug-in should they need to.

1   You can provide a video sequence in a Web page using the HTML sequence: <A HREF= "1video.rm">Click here to see the video</A> Ensure the video file has the correct filename extension for the type of video file. Or, you may be able to use the <EMBED> tag in your HTML document. See your HTML guide for more details.

2   (Optional) With modern Web page design software, the task is usually much easier than in Step 1. See the appropriate documentation for precise instructions.

3   (Optional) Include any other HTML attributes – for example, video playing position, the number of times the video sequence plays and the size of the playing window.

4   Test before going live.

Once visitors click on the link on your Web page representing the RealVideo file, their operating system opens their installed RealVideo player and starts to play the video sequence. The playback sequence

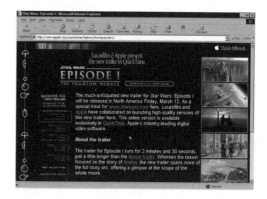

may be interrupted if significant Internet congestion is present. Buttons are available offering fast forward, rewind and search.

Animation: top hints and tips

Having powerful animation technologies at your fingertips is a great temptation. Animation can help transform a Web site into a memorable 'exciting experience'. The key to success here though, is making the right choices; deciding what's appropriate and what isn't:

Animation is ideal when trying to put over a mass of detailed information. Information can be structured into digestible blocks that are only made visible in sequence and by the movement of a visitor's mouse.

1. If a page contains some animation sequences, tell your visitors so they won't be puzzled by gaps if they're viewing with animations turned off.

2. Often, successful animation advertising works best if you provide further compelling reasons for a visitor to stay. Perhaps use a simple interactive game or quiz to provide an incentive for a visitor to stay online and bookmark the site.

3. When covering the topic of movement, development or changing states, animation can be particularly beneficial. For example, when showing key stages in a cooking recipe; or in illustrating the biological growth of an organism; or simply to show the development cycle of a product.

Navigating a complex Web site can be made easier through animation. For example, a cheerful cartoon character could move around the screen indicating links to places of interest.

4. If the subject matter can be interpreted as boring or lacking excitement, sometimes applying creative animation techniques can spruce up a Web page and heighten interest.

5. Animation does not have to be 'loud' to be effective. Small elements like sparkles or comet-type effects can sometimes make a greater impact.

6. For Web site topics involving abstract ideas and concepts or which may be difficult to visualise, animation techniques can offer a welcome boost.

7. Consider carefully the use of animated games and humour on a site which deals with sensitive issues.

Key hints on what not to animate

There's no simple answer about what not to animate. My guess is that you already know much about the type of visitor you expect to visit your Web pages. This knowledge helps define how to approach designing them. Only you, the Web page designer, really know what is best for your site and for your visitors – although often this is a learning experience. Consider the following points:

- Keep the Home/Index page 'pure'. Large animated elements create additional download time, so may not be appreciated by visitors who may be unsure that your site contains what they're looking for.

- Don't animate a page simply because you know how to and enjoy creating animations! Usually, it's better to let the purpose of a page dictate its content.

- Visitors essentially seeking information, and who become distracted by inappropriate animated elements, may become so irritated that they leave. Enticing a visitor to return after a 'bad' experience is much harder than trying to win over a new visitor.

- If the central important message of a Web page is text- or graphic-based, including animated elements will probably not help but only confuse the issue.

1 This organisation has chosen a simple, clean, uncluttered style.

2 The blue underline for links has been removed providing a clearer view.

3 Stylish shadow-type rollover buttons provide a touch of uniqueness.

Utilising 'power' components

This chapter explores some of the options open to you to make your Web site more interactive, helpful and useful to visitors. We also cover how you can password-protect a Web site or limit access to specific pages.

Covers

Chapter Eleven

Adding a drop-down 'Go' menu

A drop-down menu is an ideal way to provide multiple choice or navigation options within a small space. A drop-down menu can be activated simply by making a choice or by making a choice plus clicking a 'Go' button or something similar. Arguably, omitting the 'Go' button provides a more professional finish.

1 A drop-down menu is an excellent way to provide multiple options within a small physical space.

2 This helpful drop-down menu is provided on a fast-loading Home/ Index page.

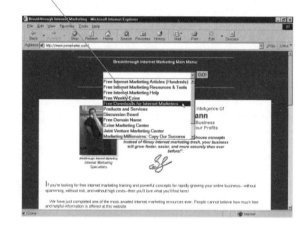

For NetObjects Fusion 4.0 users, a Go-menu Component comes with the package. Or you can purchase the more powerful LinkMaster – a JavaScript-based add-on Component – from www.coolmaps.com. This means that creating a drop-down Go-type menu that works first time is simple. And you don't need to know JavaScript: just follow the simple and clear instructions.

If you're not using NetObjects Fusion, or you're feeling more adventurous, you can create a 'Go' drop-down menu using your own JavaScript or a CGI script.

Some generous Web site providers make their scripts free for anyone to use or adapt (see the tip); check the small print and make sure you have the right to use them.

For example, take a look at Matt's script archives at:

www. worldwidemart .com/ scripts/

or:

www.javscriptsource .com/

Including a Web site Search box

For a growing Web site, one of the most useful tools you can provide is an easy Web site search tool. You can do this using a special CGI script or through JavaScript. Many free sources exist on the Net from which you can download the code and adapt it for your Web site (get permission first).

Some Web design software may include pre-designed 'Components' that can make the job much easier. Example: the SiteSearch Component from www.coolmaps.com for NetObjects Fusion v4.0 provides an easy-to-install JavaScript-based search tool that runs on the Web browser.

Atomz's fast and powerful Search system.

Currently, for most Web sites that contain fewer than 500 pages, Atomz – one of the most popular Search services – provide their powerful search tool free of charge. For more information, visit: www.atomz .com/

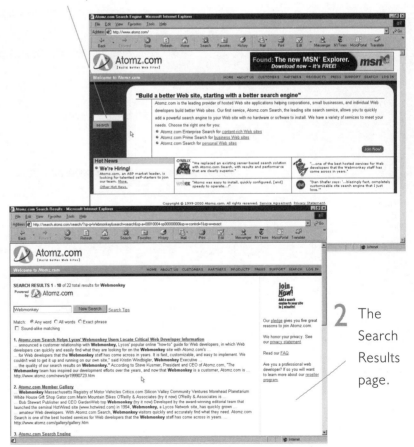

2 The Search Results page.

Creating a Sitemap page

The more pages that make up a Web site, the harder and more confusing site navigation may become for your visitors. You can make site navigation on larger sites easier using a Sitemap or Table of Contents page. Some of the better Web design software tools may also include pre-designed 'Components' for easy creation of a Sitemap page or Web site Table of Contents.

Microsoft FrontPage includes a superb Table of Contents 'FrontPage Component' that can easily create titles and text links for every page in a Web site. The SiteMap Component from www.coolmaps.com for NetObjects Fusion v4.0 also provides an easy-to-install JavaScript-based Sitemap tool that loads quickly and runs on the visitor's Web browser.

Sitemap pages provide quick access to all pages in a Web site

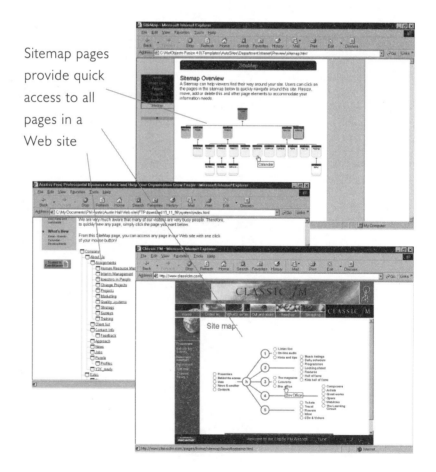

Prompting with a pop-up box

To add a special type of interactivity to a Web site, you can add a pop-up box that 'pops up' overlaid on the existing browser window when a visitor clicks a specific link, visits a particular page, or runs their mouse over an object.

For example, you could arrange for a 'Welcome' pop-up box to display. A visitor could then read the brief marketing message or details of a special promotion, then click the OK button to cause the main Home/Index page to appear.

Visitors can become irritated if the same pop-up box keeps appearing while they navigate a site. Therefore, limit the number of times a pop-up box appears to no more than 2.

However, use pop-up boxes with consideration: they can irritate visitors if too many pop-up instances occur. Ask yourself whether your choice really adds value. Coolmaps.com provide their JavaScript-based PopRocket Component for NetObjects Fusion 4.x Web design software to make the job of creating pop-up windows simple:

If you're using a Web site entry pop-up box, don't force regular visitors to view this box each time they log on: why not use cookies that automatically allow repeat visitors to bypass the box?

1 For a JavaScript-based pop-up, you'll need to include the JavaScript script between the <HEAD> and </HEAD> tags in the page from which the pop-up box originates from.

2 Enter the desired height and width settings in the Script to ensure the pop-up box is the size and shape you want.

3 Next, you create your pop-up page containing the information that you want to put in the pop-up box.

4 Save your changes. Start your Web browser and test the pop-up. You may need to repeat these steps a few times to ensure your pop-up performs the way you want.

Plug-ins, viewers and helpers

A bewildering range of file types exist designed to work with special file formats, like those from Microsoft Word, PowerPoint, Excel and perhaps ODBC database files.

To ensure their files are available to as many people as possible, many providers have created plug-ins, file viewers and helper applications that work with a Web browser to allow certain files to be made available on the Web.

To find out more about using Adobe Acrobat files, point your Web browser at: http:// www.adobe.com/

Plug-ins are available for a wide range of file types. These include Real.com's RealPlayer G2; Macromedia's Shockwave and Flash; Adobe Acrobat files; Apple's QuickTime; RealSpace FlashPix; Headspace Beatnik files; and Cosmo (a virtual reality tool), to name but a few.

Maintaining a true reproduction of the original

Imagine you want to make available on your Web site (exactly as it appears in print) a company brochure or desktop published story.

Plug-ins are available for different platforms. Make sure your visitors understand that they'll need the correct browser plug-in for their particular operating system.

If the choice of font and exact layout is particularly important, one option is to convert your brochure or other document to Adobe's Acrobat Portable Document Format (.PDF).

PDF includes all the essential information to create an electronic representation of an original document, following the same layout and choice of fonts. PDF files are compact, portable and can be viewed on a wide range of different platforms.

How plug-ins work at the browser end

Using your chosen Web design software, you insert a special document into a Web page; this is identified as a small picture or icon after you've published your Web page to the Web.

To view the special document, visitors then click the icon to have the file download to their PC or appear in their browser. However, for this to happen they must have the correct plug-in for their browser and operating system.

Dealing with unusual file formats

Firstly, if possible, try to avoid providing information in an unusual format: often, these types of files can be converted to more 'standard' formats. However, if that is not an option for you, consider the steps below:

1 Learn about the particular plug-in you want to use. Often, the best way of doing this is to point your browser at the Home page of the specific plug-in provider. Here you can glean a lot of useful information and possibly advice.

If you include these links to plug-in providers, ideally make their link open a second browser window so they will still have access to your site in the first browser window.

Why send visitors directly away from your site after you've spent much time and effort getting them to visit in the first place?

2 Insert the plug-in content onto your desired Web page using the <EMBED> tag and its attributes in HTML. See your HTML guide for details on the exact syntax to use.

3 Mention the name of the unusual format used and optionally provide some brief background information on your Web page, so visitors can access more information.

4 To provide the means whereby your visitors can view or use files stored in unusual formats, it's essential to provide a link to the Web site containing the plug-in application a visitor needs to view these unusual files.

5 Ensure the Web link address you provide in Step 4 is valid and up to date: test it regularly by downloading the file yourself and running the application.

6 Provide brief but clear instructions on what a visitor has to do to view or to use any unusual files or documents provided on your Web pages.

How www.grc.com provide access to their PDF user guide:

The SpinRite 5.0 Brochure
This four page brochure provides a quick overview of SpinRite 5.0's major features, benefits, and capabilities.
● Download this ZIPPED Adobe Acrobat 3.0 file. (28 Kbytes)
● Download this PLAIN Adobe Acrobat 3.0 file. (43 Kbytes)

Quick 'n easy JavaScript solutions

All of the special effects or 'Components' listed on this page use third-party pre-built mini-applications, usually using JavaScript. But why re-invent the wheel? With Components from www.coolmaps.com for NetObjects Fusion v4.x Web design software, you don't need to know JavaScript and they're reliable, easy to install and use. Here's some information on just a few Components.

Lots of JavaScript routines are already available on the Web. Many are free, but make sure you have permission to use them first. For example, take a look at: www. javascriptsource .com

Uploading and linking to files the easy way

The FileAway Component lets you easily and quickly upload and link to various files. First, you simply install the Component, then tell FileAway the types of files you're using and their folders/directories. FileAway automatically provides links to these files on your page. The Component then uploads these files to your Web site server (PC) located at your Web host's premises. That's it!

Control how pop-up windows behave

JavaScript pop-up windows can now be tamed with the RemoteControl Component. You can also arrange for a 'remote control' window to pop-up and stay on top of the main window! Great for advertising but can irritate users.

Both www. Coolmaps. com and NetObjects Fusion provide excellent tutorials and problem-solving support from their Web sites. See:
* *www.coolmaps .com/*
* *www.netobjects .com/*

Display random images

Have your Web site update itself automatically. To arrange for a different image to appear each time a visitor loads a page, or have an image change after a specific time delay, you can use the RandomActs Component.

Providing a Web SlideShow

In a Web slideshow, you can arrange for an image to change when a visitor clicks on another button or location on the page. A visitor can cycle forwards and backwards through a series of images. Great for showing the family holiday snaps or a range of products! The SlideShow Component from www.coolmaps.com does exactly that.

Change an image when a mouse glides over it

Give your Web site instant style. The RollOver Component can not only change its own image but also other selected images. It can change the 'roll-off' delay time as well!

Inserting a dynamic calendar onto a Web page

Never forget another date! Using the Coolmaps.com BlindDate Component, you can insert a basic calendar. You can choose dates up to 1 year in advance and link to special pages that can describe events on those dates.

Place a date and time digital clock on a page

You can use the OClock Component to quickly place a date and time clock anywhere on your page and set the time to your own time zone. Visitors see the current time in your time zone. Uses graphics not text.

Take a look at Matt's script archive at: www. worldwidemart .com/ scripts/ for lots of PERL CGI scripts (many free) that you can use to enhance your Web pages.

For lots more help in creating a Web site (whether you're just starting or a seasoned pro) point your browser at: www.projectcool. com/

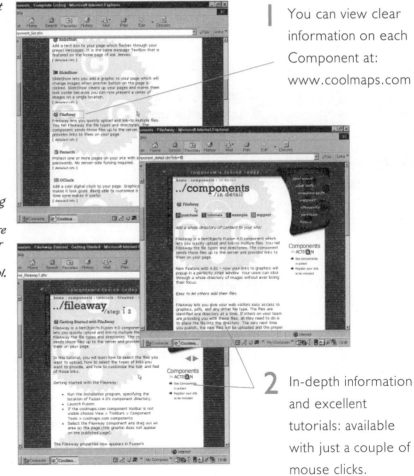

You can view clear information on each Component at: www.coolmaps.com

2 In-depth information and excellent tutorials: available with just a couple of mouse clicks.

Password-protecting your Web site

If you provide pages containing sensitive, special, important or up-to-date information, you may want to provide access on a subscription basis, or give access to authorised persons only – like employees. Using password-based access systems, you can lock out a single page, a series of pages, an entire group of pages or even an entire Web site.

For low security options, you can use a JavaScript option designed using off-the-shelf Web design software.

One simple low-security solution for NetObjects Fusion v4.x users

ProtectIT is a NetObjects Fusion 4.x Component from www.coolmaps.com that provides a quick and simple solution to password-protecting specific pages. Currently, you can create up to 20 passwords per page and, with a little imagination, you could create a system that ensures passwords are changed at regular or irregular intervals, to build a higher level of security.

Web site security in Microsoft FrontPage

In combination with the FrontPage Personal Web Server or the Microsoft Personal Web Server through the Administration commands, you can set up what FrontPage calls 'Permissions' to allow Administrator, Author and Browsing access rights. See your FrontPage guide.

Security-critical options

For a high security solution, you may need to have special encrypted files installed on your Web server. One solution is to use .htaccess on your Web host's servers to control access to specific files – and therefore Web pages. Discuss options with your Web host and liaise closely with them.

Providing a discussion forum

What is a discussion forum

People love to talk, don't they? As an essentially communication-oriented species, it's in our nature, so why not make use of that trait to benefit and enhance your Web site? Many already do this quite successfully – and profitably! But, there's a trade-off: the need for setup time and regular management and monitoring.

Creating a discussion forum can be one of the best ways to build an online community, meet new friends and forge new business associates.

A discussion forum, discussion group or bulletin board allows many visitors to submit information, views, ideas and talents onto a Web page for the benefit of others (and themselves, through the exchange of expertise and marketing benefits); these can be viewed, commented on or replied to as necessary.

How to set up a discussion forum

Establishing a discussion forum is one of the best ways to encourage visitors to return. Those visitors who do contribute to your discussion forum are obviously interested in your field, so these people may represent hot prospects for your product or service.

The best discussion forums ensure that you can closely monitor what is being said so that, if necessary, you can delete undesirable content and remove offenders from the list quickly.

Web design software from Microsoft FrontPage and NetObjects Fusion contains easy to use commands that enable you to set up discussion forum Web pages. However, liaise closely with your Web host or Internet Service Provider as you'll probably need to use their CGI scripts (or FrontPage Server Extensions if appropriate). Many Web hosts provide a discussion forum as an optional part of their Web hosting package. Take a look at: www.bigtalker.com/ and www.ultrascripts.com/

Publishing your database

For some organisations, it may make sense to put their entire database on the Web. For example, you might have thousands of product lines that you sell from your Web site with an inventory that changes daily: an ideal situation that probably demands an online database. However, this can be a particularly complex task, has clear security implications and should be considered carefully only after thorough investigation of the benefits, risks and drawbacks.

You can find many sources on the Net to help you learn more about database programming and decide the best solution for your particular needs. Plus, as software products become more user-friendly working with Web databases is becoming ever easier!

Evaluating your options

Unless you're familiar with database design and have programming skills in a language such as PERL or mySQL, you'll need to spend many hours learning how to achieve each stage, or hire a competent programmer to do the work for you. Good database programmers, however, can be costly but essential if online databasing of your product line is the path you choose. Sometimes, you can save some money by doing some of the work in-house.

1   You may not even need a full-blown database. Links 2.0 is a superb set of highly customisable scripts from which you can create a hierarchical structure. For more information, see: http://www.gossamer-threads.com/scripts/links/

NetObjects Fusion v4.x supports database production through Allaire ColdFusion or Microsoft ASP without the need to write your own JScript or VBScript.

2   Otherwise, establish whether to host your Web site on a UNIX/Linux or a Windows NT server. Creating a database in NT is usually easier than using Linux, but is normally more costly. Also, NT is considered by some to be less robust.

3   Prefer the UNIX/Linux option? Choose PERL, ePERL or PHP scripts and commands to create your database.

4   If you choose NT, you could use Cold Fusion from Allaire to develop your database. Or you could opt for Microsoft Active Server Pages (ASP) using Java or Visual Basic. Whichever you choose, your server must be compatible with it or have the necessary 'extensions' installed.

Gaining information with online forms

A Web form is a great information gatherer and all-round communications tool for both users and providers. Here, you can learn the basics about Web forms and what you need to do to include various examples in your Web site.

Covers

Chapter Twelve

Why use Web forms?

A Web form is a powerful tool for any Web site and enables three important actions to take place on a Web page:

- Interactivity: a form allows direct interaction.

- Valuable user-related information can be gathered.

- Collected information can be processed and returned to the Web page provider, usually by automated email.

Businesses, therefore, can fulfil two essential necessities:

- Gathering the right kind of data. Accurate, key marketing-related information is now so valuable, it has become a new kind of global currency.

- Receiving focused feedback about goods, services and Web site-related issues such as Web site useability, content relevancy and so on.

If you want to include forms in your Web pages, ask your ISP/Web host which services and scripts they provide for processing forms. 'Mailto', 'formmail' and 'SendMail' are three such popular scripts.

You can of course use a simple email link to meet both of the above goals. For many, this approach may be adequate. However, carefully designed forms take the load of visitors and can deliver much more focused results. To make full use of raw emailed data, you may need to extract and categorise the essentials and re-enter the data elsewhere, probably using further software tools. All this takes time. With a carefully constructed form this automatic process makes the task much easier.

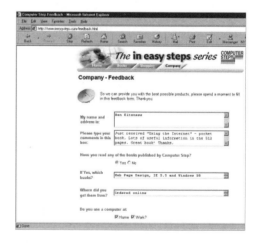

The use of forms for processing Web transactions is also becoming commonplace now that Internet users are more relaxed about leaving sensitive information like credit card details online while using secure servers (see Chapter 14).

How Web forms work

Web forms have two main components:

- The visible part – into which visitors enter data.

- The invisible component – processes entered data and may store it in a database for easy access; often achieved using a CGI script or Form handler (below).

A CGI script is a computer program which completes a task or series of related tasks and which ignores any outside intervention.

Once a visitor has completed entering data into a Web form and clicked the Submit/Send button, the data is sent, stored and processed on the Web Forms server

CGI scripts can carry out a range of other valuable tasks on a Web page. For example: fast-changing data such as stocks and shares can be displayed and updated on-the-fly.

For more information, speak to your ISP, Web host or CGI-programmer.

```
                    <TD WIDTH=62><IMG SRC="../../../clearpixel.gif" WIDTH=62 HEIGHT=1 BORDER=0></TD>
                <TD></TD>
            </TR>
            <TR VALIGN=TOP ALIGN=LEFT>
                <TD HEIGHT=24></TD>
                <TD WIDTH=70>
<!--<INPUT TYPE=SUBMIT NAME="ClubMailer4.111" VALUE="Submit" ID="ClubMailer4.111">
-->
<INPUT TYPE="hidden" NAME="SiteName" VALUE="phenneger-morgan.com">
<INPUT TYPE="hidden" NAME="FormName" VALUE="SeminarRegistrationForm">
<INPUT TYPE="hidden" NAME="SenderID" VALUE="2629">
<INPUT TYPE="hidden" NAME="Sender" VALUE="pminfo@phenneger-morgan.com">
<INPUT TYPE="hidden" NAME="Subject" VALUE="Thank you for the registration.">
<INPUT TYPE="hidden" NAME="FormResultURL" VALUE="http://www.phenneger-morgan.com/ESOPs/Seminars/Agen
<INPUT TYPE="hidden" NAME="CM_ReturnMail" VALUE="Yes">
<INPUT TYPE="hidden" NAME="CM_ReturnMail_CCSender" VALUE="No">
<INPUT TYPE="hidden" NAME="Recipient" VALUE="pminfo@phenneger-morgan.com,webmaster@phenneger-morgan.
<INPUT TYPE=SUBMIT VALUE="Submit">
</TD>
                <TD></TD>
                <TD WIDTH=72><INPUT TYPE=RESET NAME="FormsButton1" VALUE="Cancel" ID="FormsButto
            </TR>
        </TABLE>
    </FORM>
```

An extract of HTML used in a Web form

usually by carrying out the instructions in the CGI script. The CGI establishes how entered information is routed to the Forms server (a powerful PC) and how the resulting data is routed back to a user's Web browser for confirmation.

Scripting options

Some Web hosts/ISPs support various kinds of Web form processing scripts as part of their standard service. The well known Internet Service Provider Demon, for example, supports at least four basic types of script: forms processing, forms test script, page counter and 'clickable' graphics. With some Web hosts/ISPs, you can pay for these extra services! Some may not support any scripting services, so check before signing up with a new Web host.

A script can be written in a variety of computer languages. However, as scripts are hosted on an ISP's servers, many ISPs offer script writing services. Or, you can make arrangements to provide your own script which meets your Web host's criteria. Ensure the script writer liaises closely with your Web host to avoid an expensive 'clean up' bill!

Basic form components

A Web form can be simple or complex. The more complex, the more finely-tuned can be your responses: precise rather than vague information has immense value. Web forms contain simple elements or building blocks, including:

- Text entry boxes: space for a limited amount of text.

- Hidden fields: similar to text entry boxes, except each character entered is displayed as an asterisk (*) to keep sensitive information private.

- Check boxes: to indicate one or more chosen options. A check box can be On (box ticked) or Off (box clear). Several check boxes can be used at any one time.

- Radio buttons: allow one of several options to be chosen. When a radio button is 'On', all others in the related group are turned 'Off'.

- Pop-up menus and scrolling menus: provide menu choices either as a fully displayed block or as multiple options made available through a scrollable list.

- Plain push-buttons: include two basic renamable HTML types. SUBMIT sends all data in a form to the server; RESET usually clears the form by entering default values in each field.

- Image push-buttons: a graphic or image icon instead of a plain grey box.

A Web page form need not have a plain look. If you have a series of Web pages based on a template, you may want to maintain continuity and perhaps include strong branding components or even advertisements.

However, consider the benefits and drawbacks of making a form too 'busy'.

1 Radio button.

2 Pop-up menu.

3 Text box.

...cont'd

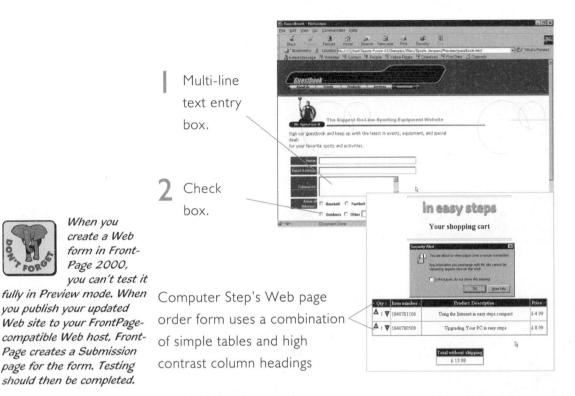

1 Multi-line text entry box.

2 Check box.

When you create a Web form in Front-Page 2000, you can't test it fully in Preview mode. When you publish your updated Web site to your FrontPage-compatible Web host, Front-Page creates a Submission page for the form. Testing should then be completed.

Computer Step's Web page order form uses a combination of simple tables and high contrast column headings

Using tables in Web forms

Table structures in a form are invaluable. Often, a Web form includes a series of fields designed to prompt a visitor to enter details or make choices: name, address, email address, etc. Consider the following guidelines:

1 Without a table structure, each field directly below the field above may not be aligned vertically, so you can end up with a series of displaced fields which looks untidy.

2 Using a table structure, all these fields can be arranged in a column aligned neatly to one edge of the window.

3 Often, Web forms use a two-column table structure with as many rows as required. You can arrange for all the field titles to be placed in the left-hand column and the fields themselves in the right-hand column for perfect alignment.

Creating an online form

You can create forms either by building the components (text boxes, radio buttons, pop-up menu lists, etc.) one step at a time using any text editor or dedicated HTML editor, or you can use one of the graphical Web design software packages (e.g. Microsoft FrontPage, NetObjects Fusion or Adobe PageMill). These packages usually include several pre-built template forms that you can use 'as is' or easily adapt to suit your needs.

Before getting started, consider the following guidelines:

Microsoft FrontPage forms use special FrontPage 'Components'. For these to work properly, your Web host must support them and have the correct FrontPage Server Extensions also installed.

1 Establish how you want to receive the form data. For information-gathering forms, you usually have several options, outlined in Steps 2, 3 and 4 below.

2 (Option) You can arrange for the form data to be copied to a text file and stored on your Web host's server.

3 (Option) Send the form data to an email address you specify.

For NetObjects Fusion 4.x users, www.coolmaps. com Club provide a forms solution. Their ClubMailer Component and service allow you to send form results by email without any need to involve your Web host.

4 (Option) Use a CGI-script or Form Handler Component stored on your Web host's server to perform further processing and actions on the information in your form and perhaps display a Confirmation/Thank you page to your visitor. Discuss options with your Web host as your forms and their servers must work together and talk the same language.

5 Most good Web hosts now provide a CGI-bin for their customers. A CGI-bin is essentially a storage location that may contain various standard scripts that can be used to process your forms. Common CGI scripts include formmail.pl and mailto.exe. If you use these services, ensure compatibility with your software.

Preventing bad input data

Unless you install some kind of automatic checking procedure, it may be possible for a visitor to enter the wrong information in the wrong field, or simply enter irrelevant information. For example, in a name field you usually wouldn't want a visitor to enter numbers. To prevent this kind of problem, you could ensure that your name field only accepts upper- and lower-case letters.

Or when using date fields, for example, you might want visitors to use a specific date format like dd/mm/yy or mm/dd/yyyy so that when you receive this information you can import it easily into, say, a database program of some kind.

Although form validation can be done with CGI on your Web server, JavaScript running on the visitor's PC usually performs the task much faster.

Sometimes, you might want to ensure that a visitor must enter information into specific fields in order to submit the form, or you might not want any blank fields submitted. If you're providing a free ezine containing high value information, most people might consider that providing basic contact details is a fair exchange.

For lots of really useful (and often free) JavaScripts, take a look at: www.javascriptsource .com/

You just need to ensure that they provide all the information you ask, but try to make the process as quick and painless as possible to ensure a maximum sign-up rate. You then know that those who have signed up may also be hot prospects for your product or service, if you provide one.

How to prevent bad input data

Usually, the most effective solution is to use a JavaScript routine. You can find many free snippets of code from generous providers on the Web (example: see the HOT TIP). Or if you use NetObjects Fusion, FormValidator is a great Component from www.coolmaps.com that does exactly what we've discussed.

Installing a guestbook

Providing a guestbook form is a popular option for many Web site owners. For those creating a personal Web site, it's simply nice to interact and get to know your visitors, meet new friends – and hopefully gain some feedback about your Web site.

For businesses, interaction and feedback with your visitors is essential. Any mechanism that you can add to your Web site to legally and morally capture an email address is money well spent (see the tip). A guestbook form is one option.

 Visitors can receive thousands of irrelevant emails each year. This 'email spam' wastes their time and resources and so understandably can raise strong emotions. Protect your visitor's email address and include a Privacy statement/page demonstrating your commitment.

When recording information about people, remember to check possible obligations with the Data Protection Registrar (www.open .gov.uk/dpr/dprhome.htm).

Creating a guestbook Web page

Although you can use raw HTML to build a guestbook page, many current Web design software packages provide pre-built guestbook templates that you can edit or adapt to suit your needs using simple to use menu commands.

Microsoft FrontPage, NetObjects Fusion and HotMetal Pro include a range of form types including guestbook templates.

In fact, Microsoft FrontPage also provides additional form templates: feedback, confirmation, user registration and even a form 'Wizard' to help you create those unusual, unique and sometimes tricky form designs.

Providing a feedback form

After putting in much time and effort to create a great Web site, it's easy to think you've done everything correctly. However, what you may find easy, others may not, and vice versa. One of the most beneficial things you can do to build a trusting relationship with your visitors is to ask them what they think about your Web site:

- Does it meet their needs?

- Is it easy to use?

- What more would they like to see?

- And so on.

 Don't ask for too much information though: visitors may feel this is too intrusive. Striving to find the right balance is always worthwhile.

Some statistics suggest that a visitor is twice as likely to fill in a feedback form than click on an email link to send you a message. Key point: a simple and well designed Web form is easier and quicker to use than an email program.

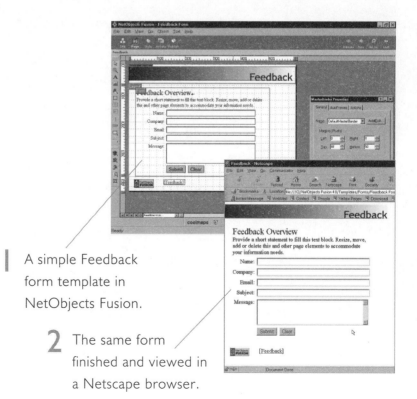

| A simple Feedback form template in NetObjects Fusion.

2 The same form finished and viewed in a Netscape browser.

Web forms: top design hints and tips

1   Test a newly designed form using several different Web browsers to ensure maximum compatibility.

2   You can easily set up a form to handle simple enquiries, sign up for an ezine, or to gain feedback information. Your ISP or Web host may provide a form script that exactly meets your needs! However, you'll probably need to enter the email address to which you want the form information sent.

3   You can include a separate form 'inside' another so each form collects and sends distinct information to the server. Although a powerful technique, nesting forms in this way can sometimes confuse visitors and is therefore probably best avoided, unless you have a strong reason to include multiple forms.

Adding pizazz to your Web form buttons

If you want to add a little uniqueness to your form design, instead of using the usual boring grey-coloured Submit buttons, consider using an image button instead:

1   Create your button images in a program like Paint Shop Pro or NetStudio.

2   Then, instead of using the usual HTML code:
```
<INPUT type="submit" value="Subscribe">
```
enter the following:

```
<INPUT TYPE="image" value="Subscribe" SRC="images/subscribe.gif">
```

Remember: substitute the example SRC path above with yours, so that it points to where your new Subscribe button (or other button) image is located.

Designing your Web pages

Just adding some text and one or two ill-considered pictures doesn't create an effective Web page. In this chapter, we cover the essentials that you need to know and how to create some special types of Web pages.

Covers

Chapter Thirteen

Creating effective Web page titles

To help get best results in the search engines listings, keep your Title between 50-70 characters in length and place it directly after the opening <HEAD> tag and before any META descriptions, keywords, or JavaScript code.

Why Web page titles are so important

The title of a Web page is what appears in the Browser window Title bar when you access a Web page. The Web page title is *absolutely essential* to a higher ranking in search engines and directories.

Carefully considered title from the highly successful Cellwest.com

The power words: 'You', 'New' and 'Free' almost always get our attention. Use them often in your Web pages for best results.

MOST IMPORTANT: Make sure your title fulfils the following conditions: (1) Is meaningful, (2) Contains your number 1 keyword (see the facing page) which is *not* the first word in your title, and (3) It describes your Unique Selling Proposition (USP) – i.e. it clearly and quickly demonstrates why someone should choose or buy from you above anyone else.

Creating your Web page titles

Key point: try to make your first word low in the Alphabet or as close to 'A' as possible. Some search engines use alphabetical listing systems, so 'A's get listed first etc.

Consider the following page title:

'Welcome to gardening.com'

This contains 24 characters including spaces (excluding quotes included here for clarity); it's short, snappy but doesn't include a key benefit. Perhaps a better title could be:

'Access free gardening tips and great value gardening supplies'

This is longer with 61 characters including spaces but it's more meaningful and includes two BENEFITS.

META tags for better exposure

META tags allow you to include special extra information about a Web page that is normally invisible to visitors but which can nevertheless be seen by browsers and search engines. Lots of different META tags are available, but here we'll examine the two most important ones: the Keyword tag and Description tag.

To check out the 200 most popular keywords people search for at Yahoo, go to: http://eyescream.com/yahootop200.html (Warning: some words reflect adult themes.)

META tags are similar to HTML tags, except you place all META tags between the <HEAD> and </HEAD> HTML tags in your Web pages. You can manually place META tags in each of your Web pages or use the easy commands often available in Web design software packages. To form a better picture of the keyword META tag, here's the basic structure:

<META name="keywords" content="widgets,Widget user guide">

The META description tag

In the 'content' section of the description META tag, you simply enter a carefully constructed and brief description of the Web page/site; consider the guidelines below. Here's the basic structure of the Description META tag:

<META name="description" content="Yourname.com's guide to designing your own Widgets!">

The considered use of Web titles, descriptions and keywords as described in these pages is one of the best ways to bring free visitor traffic to your Web site.

Consider the following guidelines:

1 Keep it plain and simple; include your Unique Selling Proposition (USP). Avoid blatant self-promotion, repeating keywords or brand names (unless they're yours).

2 Create several descriptions of your Web site: one containing fewer than 5 words, another about 25 words, and another with about 50 words. Why? Some search engines/directories want a brief description; others allow longer descriptions.

3 Double-check your spelling and grammar, then save this information in a plain text file (.txt) for easy copying into search engines/directories later.

The HTML for the Web page shown on page 130:

Don't try to repeat the same keyword many times over or try to hide it in a page using the same colour as the page background. Search engines are aware of this trick; if they detect it they may severely reduce your page ranking or even refuse to list your Web site.

1 Page Title.

2 META description.

Using META tags to apply copyright to a page

You can use the copyright META tag to identify yourself or your organisation as copyright holder. Modify the example below with your information:

<META name="copyright" content="This page and all its contents are copyright 1999-2000 by Brian Austin. All Rights Reserved Worldwide.">

Rather than try to outwit the search engines and directories, and risk getting permanently low ranked or even banned, why not just work with them. Find out their rules/conditions for listing and abide by them. Just use every reasonable technique you can to improve your site's ranking.

A range of META tags is available to enable you to control more precisely how search engines can access your Web site

Assembling your META keywords/phrases

Consider the highly valuable tips on the facing page to help make your Web site ranking soar! Follow them precisely. Be patient and persistent and apply the techniques in combination with other guidelines in this book.

Search engines: top keyword tips

Key information provided in these few pages is regularly sold by Internet consultants for hundreds of times the cost of this book – and most Web sites still don't apply such careful techniques! Your astute book choice now puts you as a Web designer in an incredibly unique and powerful position, but ONLY if you apply these techniques. Congratulations!

1   Arrange keywords/phrases in order of importance, the most important first, separated by commas, *no spaces between keywords*; shortened example: <META name="keywords" content="free help,online marketing,internet marketing">.

2   Make sure the first 200 words of text on your page contain the keywords you use in: (1) your Web page title, (2) description and (3) keywords as described in this section.

3   Choose keywords carefully! Make a 'rough' list of the kinds of words and phrases you think people might enter in a search engine to find your Web site. Include some common misspellings: many people have problems with spelling; also consider international spelling differences.

4   Make a 'fine' list of about 40-50. Then choose about 10 from that list that you consider are the most important. Keep a copy of both lists in a plain text (.txt) file on your PC's hard drive: then you have easy access for copy/pasting later.

Here's why you should usually use phrases instead of single words. Current search engines can pick out single words but can't put together phrases made up of your single words.

5   When possible, use keyword phrases and plurals instead of single words: 'consultants' is better than 'consultant' Why? Because 'consultants' will pick up 'consultant' and 'consult' as well. Get the idea?

6   Appreciate that you can dilute your keyword mix simply by having too many! Have as few keywords as you can. Why? The more keywords you have, the higher the relevance each remaining keyword may be given in a search engine.

7   ESSENTIAL: Don't repeat a keyword more than once. Search engines may consider this to be keyword spamming and automatically heavily reduce your ranking.

8   Avoid putting banners, tables, graphics or any other 'obstacles' at the top of a page: put keyword-rich text there.

Creating compelling content

Essentially a Web site is a just another type of publication: an electronic brochure. So what you put in makes a difference. Consider thinking of your Web site not as a Web site, but as a stimulating experience! This might seem like an unlikely proposition, but there are Web sites out there doing just that!

Generally, people don't like to read text on a screen – if given the choice. Therefore, simply work with this trait and aim to keep text paragraphs brief, clear and to the point.

Key point: if your *target* visitors find your Web pages interesting, attractive and compelling, they're more likely to revisit and recommend your site to others. If they revisit, you have further chances to state your case, start a dialogue, make a friend, or close a sale. And personal recommendations are always the best way to build trust.

Deciding what to include in your pages

Once you've clearly established your marketing goals and developed a plan, consider the following ideas:

1 Visitors read only what interests them or is relevant to them. Design your pages to match.

Include a brief description for each image used: search engines can 'see' the contents of the ALT tags in images (Chapter 7).

2 Try to provide some free content: the word FREE has a lot of power and people just love it!

3 Create attractive content that is appropriate for your target visitors.

4 Experiment with ideas to describe your products and services in a compelling and eye-catching way.

5 Empty space on a Web page can work for you – the 'considered' choice of empty space is not empty but 'active'.

6 Although lots of attention-seeking components are available, sometimes a clean, uncluttered Web page can carry its own message.

7 Avoid overloading a page with too much information. If necessary, spread the information over several pages.

Using humour

Jokes and cartoons, tastefully portrayed, can add final touches to a Web page – or form the central theme of a Web site if you're in the laughter business. However, humour needs careful handling. Consider the following:

1 To encourage feedback, you could try monthly joke contests with prizes – ideally products from the Web site – for the winners.

2 Or perhaps a competition to find the funniest, most unusual, or striking email address.

The Home page represents an ideal point at which to fire peoples' imaginations, engage their brains, provide drama or make an impact!

3 Here's another successful idea: invite visitors to email, in 50 words or fewer, why they think they deserve a free [product]. Then publish the results. I suspect some hilarious offerings could be forwarded in these situations offering high entertainment value to all concerned.

4 Treat humour-based content with special respect: your brand of humour may not be shared. What you consider funny, others might see as offensive. If you're unsure, get second opinions, or simply choose another approach.

This Web site seems to find the humour balance perfectly

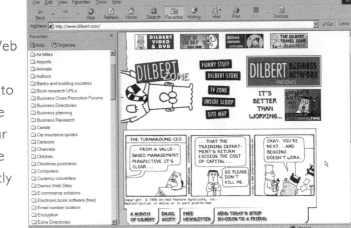

A generic Home/Index page

The Home page is a little like the front door of your house: it's one of the main components your visitors see when they log on to your Web site. Your Home/Index page should clearly state within the first few sentences what your Web site is about. For businesses, a Home page can also be likened to the front cover of a brochure, sales literature, a newsletter or a magazine.

The Home/ Index page is the best place to remind visitors to book-mark your site. In fact, also remind them in a couple of additional places as well.

Deciding what to include in a Home page is crucial. Sometimes, there's a great temptation to include far more than perhaps we should. In fact, often we can create a better Home page by establishing what to leave out *after* deciding what we think we need to include.

To avoid overloading visitors with too much clutter at 'Your front door', it's a good idea to limit the number of distinct information chunks to no more than 10 on the Home page – fewer if possible. This helps create a feeling of space and puts over a sense of planned expectation. Consider:

Ideally, create a browser-independent Web site. But if specific types of browser are essential to view your Web site, tell your visitors which browser(s) work best when viewing your Web pages.

1 Keep the amount of content on the Home/Index page to a minimum. Your Home/Index page is a kind of filter to the other pages that make up your Web site.

2 If possible, include an ezine sign-up box, a guestbook link or a feedback link box. Or consider other ways in which you can capture a visitor's email address.

3 This Home page provides a clean, uncluttered look.

4 A single, high quality animated GIF provides an interactive component.

A personal Home page

A 'personal' Web page performs a different purpose to that of club or business-related Web sites, and should therefore include only relevant components appropriate to their design.

Some of the best Web pages have been developed by individuals who want to promote their hobby or interest and connect with other like-minded individuals. In this way, the Web can produce and stimulate the development of many smaller 'communities'.

 Your Web space may not cost anything if you already have an email account! Many Internet Service Providers make some free Web space available for you to use should you choose to. Speak to your ISP for details.

1 Basic text links.

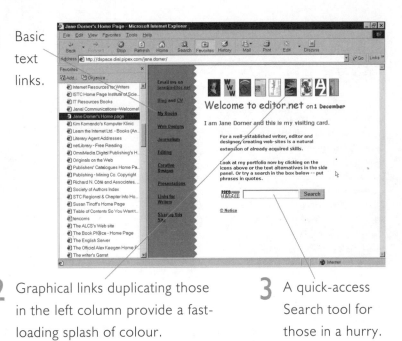

2 Graphical links duplicating those in the left column provide a fast-loading splash of colour.

3 A quick-access Search tool for those in a hurry.

Creating a twenty-four hour online CV

In a personal Web site, you can let your creative flair blossom. In fact, some individuals use a personal Web site as a kind of curriculum vitae.

Many others at least include their CV as one of their Web pages. An online CV can provide a powerful demonstration of your abilities and imagination. If you include a photo, capture the real you: consider using a photo that puts over warmth. A passport-type photo may not achieve this goal!

1 Here a simple design is used for a CV page.

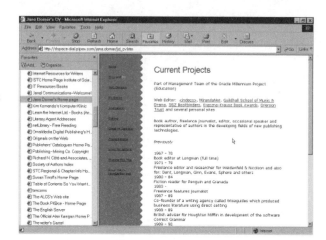

2 While on this site, the author prefers a less formal approach.

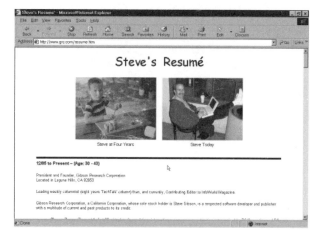

Borrow from business: adopt a theme

When designing a personal Web site, remember that, although visitors will probably expect you to talk about yourself often, the last thing they want to read is lots of *I's*. One way to avoid this situation is to design your Web pages around a theme.

For example, this could be the place where you live or a keen hobby or interest. In this way, you can captivate visitors by introducing the things that interest you before mentioning something about yourself. The more unique or unusual your theme, the more compelling it can be.

Deciding what to include

For a personal web site, you can establish what to put in your Web pages by answering two questions:

- Why are you providing a personal Web presence?

- Who is the Web page to be designed for – a section of the community or simply anyone?

As a general reference, consider the following guidelines:

- Your name and qualifications if relevant that you want to include.

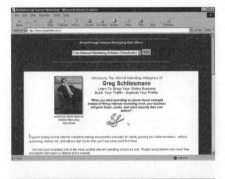

- A good photograph of yourself – choose one that is special – not a passport-type photo. If the career approach is important, consider discussing options with a professional photographer.

- First paragraph: mention the purpose of your Web page. Visitors who mistakenly navigate to your site won't waste time (and clog up your site) by having to read further.

- If you want others to contact you, display essential contact information clearly. If you have several pages, ideally include this information on each page.

- Make sure visitors can navigate easily through your Web site.

- Make your site interesting; include lots of variety.

HOT TIP

Change your content regularly and let people know that you update regularly. Ideally, include a 'What's New' type page.

A site that becomes known for regularly providing fresh content helps keep your Web site in your visitors' 'top of mind awareness' zone. Powerful. Effective!

Creating supplementary pages

Use the power of consistency to help your visitors

When considering the design aspects of supplementary pages – that is, those which link back to the Home page – it's a good idea to consider having a consistent design style throughout all your pages. Consistency across a series of Web pages helps reassure visitors in two ways:

• It provides an increased awareness that they're still on the same Web site.

• Familiar signposts mean visitors can better establish their location within the scheme of things.

The power of colours, text styles and orientation

When naming your pages, make sure all your page names are in lowercase: some Web host servers are case-sensitive. INDEX.HTML may not be considered the same as index.html or Index.html.

Colours can mean more than just colour. Why not consider a specific colour for page titles; another for subheadings, another for style of body text, and so on. This same colour scheme could be carried on to all your pages, so visitors know right from the outset what to expect. Another way in which you can help your visitors orient themselves is to place common design elements like logos, buttons or other icons in the same place from page to page.

Saying Good-Bye to 'Under Construction' signs

Avoid using 'Under Construction' signs. Visitors may not take providers of an unfinished page seriously, especially in business. If a page is not ready to put on the Web, it's arguably more professional to complete its design before uploading it to your Web site.

As a last resort, if you absolutely have to publish an unfinished page, sometimes the best approach is to simply don't advertise the fact that it is unfinished.

Providing a FAQ page

People buying products and services may have many questions to ask before deciding to buy. If you're designing a Web site that includes some level of customer support, sometimes a single Web page dedicated to answering Frequently Asked Questions (FAQs) can be a valuable aid for your visitors whilst saving you a lot of extra work. Some of the benefits of providing FAQ files include:

- They can overcome possible objections to a sale without requiring direct contact (instant cost saving).

- They demonstrate that detailed consideration has been given to customers' needs right from the outset.

- They can provide a greater range of information enabling customers to make better buying decisions.

- They can reduce the need for after-sales problem-solving support as basic questions can be answered in advance.

Microsoft FrontPage and NetObjects Fusion both include a FAQ template or Wizard.

If you can provide FAQ lists, it's usually a good idea to do so. The cost of Web space, compared with more traditional advertising media, is low and so this method offers real value for money in addition to providing quick help for your visitors.

To create a FAQ list, follow the steps below:

1 Think of common questions visitors might ask and then clearly document both the questions with the answers. If, during this exercise, other possible questions emerge, don't worry: by providing the answers, you're actually making the buying decision easier for your customers.

2 If necessary, interview sales and support staff who regularly deal with these kinds of problems to learn about the kind of questions visitors might ask.

3 Save, edit, check and convert the FAQ file to HTML format and include within your Web site.

4 Provide a link to the FAQ file, possibly on the Home page and maybe other appropriate pages too. Make sure visitors know about your FAQ pages.

Using Web page templates

For larger Web sites containing many pages, often the easiest way to be consistent in design across all the pages is to use templates which include all the common text and graphic elements you want to include on every page. Here's how:

1 First, establish all the components to be included in your template.

2 Next, create the Web page and save it as a template (ideally). Otherwise, simply save it to a location that you know is for your Web page templates.

Some of the best Web design software (including: Microsoft FrontPage, Macromedia Dreamweaver, NetObjects Fusion and HotMetal Pro) provide many different Web page and Web site templates that can save you hours of extra work.

3 When you're ready to create a page based on the template, open the template and immediately save it to another name (so you don't wipe over your original template with the changes you're about to make).

4 You can then modify the page to include all the essential details for the current page, then re-save.

5 Repeat Steps 3 and 4 for all the other pages you want to include

6 Here's the 'Service' page from the NetObjects Fusion Company Internet template.

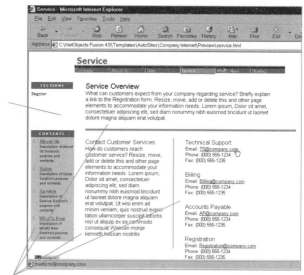

7 You simply replace the 'hint' text with your own text.

Routing to browser-specific pages

Some sophisticated Web pages may not display properly even on the most common Web browsers. However, by applying some simple techniques you can perform a check on a browser when it tries to access your Web page/site.

The free 'Browser-Matcher' script checks which browser a visitor is using and then redirects the visitor to the browser-compatible page you create. Check it out at: www.citro.net/scripts/more.shtml#browse

Then if the browser is not compatible with that page, re-route the visitor to a page that is compatible with their browser. This way, most visitors see your pages as you intended them to be seen. The drawback is of course more work for you and possibly the need to create another set of Web pages.

Using JavaScript to detect JavaScript-compatible browsers

Early browsers did not support JavaScript. If your default pages contain JavaScript and these older browsers were to try and view them, an error message would almost certainly be displayed – not a good start for a new visitor.

To edit your HTML pages and include JavaScript, I recommend you do not use word processor software as it is too easy to save the file in the software's native format.

Use a pure text editor like TextPad (Helios Software Solutions: www.textpad.com)

Adapt the code below to detect the version of JavaScript you want to optionally re-route a visitor to another page. Set the minimum version of JavaScript you want to check for in 'LANGUAGE='. If that condition is met, the visitor is re-routed to the 'welcome2.html' page, otherwise, the message between <H3> and </H3> is displayed on the page below:

```
<HTML>
<HEAD>
<TITLE>For JavaScript-compatible browsers</TITLE>
<SCRIPT LANGUAGE="JAVASCRIPT1.2"
TYPE="TEXT/JAVASCRIPT">
<!--Hides this script from older browsers
window.location="welcome2.html"
// End of hiding script from older browsers -->
</SCRIPT>
</HEAD>
<BODY BGCOLOR="BLUE">
<H3>Your Web browser is not compatible with the latest
version of JavaScript. You can upgrade using this link...</H3>
</BODY>
</HTML>
```

Creating 3D Web pages

Most Web sites currently display in two dimensions, often using a newsletter-type delivery approach. However, we see, touch and think in 3D, so it's natural to extend this to a Web page.

Arranging to view in 3D reintroduces depth and brings us back to what are arguably more natural surroundings. This has benefits for Web page designers:

For visitors to benefit fully from 3D – particularly VRML – usually a relatively fast PC is desired. I suggest at least a 133 MHz Pentium-type PC with at least 32 Mb of RAM. (A 486-based computer would probably struggle and therefore frustrate visitors.)

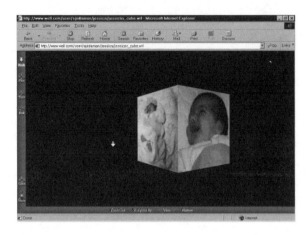

having the capability to view an object (and then turn it around to examine what it looks like from all angles) provides a much better picture of that object. For some complex objects, the ability to move in 3D could be considered essential – medical uses for example. The all-encompassing term 'object', used above, could of course be modified in other ways for use on a Web page. Consider:

• Taking an imaginary tour around a new type of car engine in a motor company Web site.

• Examining skeletal structures from all angles in a medical-oriented Web site.

• Browsing through the aisles of a virtual store, picking up goods and examining them before purchasing.

• Watching a living entity grow and mutate in a natural history oriented Web site.

• Navigating around a large University using a 3D map.

• Moving through the fascinating corridors of a top museum or picture gallery. And so on.

Virtual Reality Modelling Language

The Virtual Reality Modelling Language (VRML) is yet another computer language and emerging standard undergoing regular updates and revisions which essentially tries to simulate the way we interact with the world: in 3D!

VRML attempts to provide an imaginary space in which multiple individual components can be displayed naturally, and made to interact with and move around each other. VRML components can now be included in Web pages.

Although this technology is still relatively new, VRML is developing fast. VRML version 2.0 – affectionately called the Moving Worlds standard – includes contributions from a wide range of top software authorities and offers some exciting possibilities, including:

To participate in VRML, a visitor's browser needs to be VRML compatible. This means either having the appropriate VRML plug-in correctly installed, or using a dedicated VRML browser.

- The ability to handle a wider range of 3D environments.

- It aims to provide an open platform-independent base to encourage contributions from different technologies (Windows, Apple Mac, and so on).

- It can include animated components.

- It includes more scope for providing realistic real-world behaviour.

Including VRML in your Web pages

VRML is not currently part of HTML. To create a VRML environment, you need to use special development tools. These are available for several different platforms.

Examples include: 3D Internet Designer from Data Becker; and Virtual Home Space Builder and Internet 3D Space Builder, both from Paragraph International.

Any piece of complex new software takes time to learn. However, to ensure your Web pages stand out from the mass competing for visitors' attention, the results could be well worth the effort required. Only you can really evaluate whether 3D is right for your Web site.

VRML applications

For businesses, VRML offers special benefits that are only recently being fully realised. Access can be provided to documents, databases and many other information sources all in 3D space.

Applying VRML techniques can include the following areas of a Web site:

- Those with high entertainment value – computer games in particular have been using 3D techniques successfully in recent years.

- VRML can make Web site navigation much easier.

- Complex themes can be visualised better.

- Effective simulations can be performed, possibly saving time, money and even lives!

- VRML 3D provides a closer approximation of what 3D is attempting to simulate.

Internet Explorer users can install Microsoft's VRML v2.0 Plug in, available from the Microsoft Web site. Then when you log on to a site containing 3D content, the plug-in starts automatically.

For businesses and organisations, 3D has a natural home in the areas of:

- Retail shopping – here we can imagine the virtual supermarket concept and apply this to any business, large or small.

- Some areas of Research – complex mathematical and graphical data in particular can be presented better.

- Many areas in the world of work – some not yet defined or even realised!

- Computer-type interactive games – in fact, arguably, this area has been and still is the driving force behind 3D development.

However, often these techniques can be applied to other areas successfully and indeed the business world is quickly realising the benefits VRML and 3D can bring.

Creating a killer business Web site!

Businesses have perhaps the most to lose or gain from a Web site. So it's essential to start off properly. In this chapter, we tackle the essential issues head on.

Covers

Chapter Fourteen

For businesses: Web hot spots

The Web has enormous implications for almost any business and provides lots of exciting opportunities. Customers worldwide can have access to your product or service, twenty-four hours a day. If you're in business but do not yet have a Web site, information and guidelines in this book could benefit your business – even transform it!

Why establish a business Web site

Consider some of the reasons why many have already put their businesses on the Web:

If you provide professional advice, it's a good idea to have professional indemnity insurance to protect yourself from possible law suits. The global nature of the Web means legal repercussions of any dispute may not be clear-cut.

- There's a global reach; no national boundaries apply.

- No premises or similar rental costs are required.

- Low overheads: Web space is cheap!

- A business can be open 24 hours a day, every day.

- A Web provider has a visitor's *total* attention, in contrast to conventional sales environments.

- Sales can be increased cost-effectively.

- Gain a competitive edge: set up an effective Web site before your competitors!

- The Web and email cut marketing costs.

- By placing representations of corporate printed catalogues on a Web site, fewer conventional printed versions may be needed, creating further savings.

- Statistics show that many Internet users are affluent: a Web site can therefore provide a direct link to these potentially rich customer profiles.

- Incentives/promotions can be tested quickly, cheaply.

- Certain niche products which can't be sold cost-effectively by traditional methods may be viable on the Internet because of the low setup and running costs and the powerful global reach.

If possible, try to register several variations of your domain name, especially common misspellings. The small cost outlay for getting a domain name will almost certainly pay for itself, when you consider the possible loss of business that might result otherwise.

Establishing your domain name

Maybe not all the best domain names are taken! Network Solutions (USA), repossess thousands due to non-payment. For a tiny fee you can have a list of these names emailed to you. Check out: www.unclaimed domains.com/

What is a domain name

A domain name is the online equivalent of a mail address. Web businesses need a businesslike identity. This starts with getting a 'true' domain name. Examples of 'true' domain names include: ineasysteps.com, caade.net and AustinHall.co.uk. When you add 'http://www.' to the front of a domain name, you have a full Web address (or URL).

Get a true domain name

A 'true' domain name is much better than one derived from an Internet Service Provider's address. Consider the following two examples; one is easier to remember:

www.austinhall.co.uk

http://ourworld.compuserve.com/homepages/Austin_Hall/

Key point: usually, the shorter your domain name, the better. Include it on all business stationery. When ready, tell as many people as possible about your Web address. For international organisations, the .com – meaning company/ organisation – is the best choice. However, you could also register .net and .co.uk if they're still available.

If possible, consider registering names which sound similar to your 'main' domain (to prevent organisations that you may not want to be associated with using them).

Your potential clients may enter similar-sounding names to find you as a first measure, rather than using a search engine, simply because it's easier.

How to reserve a domain name

1 Check if the domain name you want is available (no one else has already claimed it). Go to: www.networksolutions.com/cgi-bin/whois/whois

2 If the domain name you want is still available, register it quickly! For .com, .net and .org domain names you can use: www.networksolutions.com/ The cost is currently US $70 for new registrations over 2 years; thereafter US $35 p.a.

3 For .co.uk registrations, you can use Nominet in the UK at www.nic.uk/ Cost is currently £80 + VAT, covers 2 years.

4 Network Solutions/Nominet send confirmation emails for your business records and proof of ownership. Keep copies.

Web business guidelines

For businesses the Web Search engines and Directories can:

- *provide access to a vast range of business information*
- *enable users to research existing and new markets and;*
- *even provide information about competitors*

Established businesses setting up a Web presence should consider employing experts to create a new Web brand image. Branding is often considered to be an essential component of any successful Internet business – even tiny Web ventures!

Small business Web sites

Arguably, those who have most to gain from hosting a Web site are small businesses – they can present their product or service on the same level as the larger organisations. A tiny business can project a Web image as well as, or better than, an international company: the key is the page design.

Corporate Web sites

Setting up a corporate Web site can be the most complex of all as many issues may be involved. For example, many companies have a clearly defined policy regarding the use of logos and other corporate graphic styles. Therefore, this and other such aspects should be considered early in your Web site design as part of an overall design plan.

Also, there's the aspect of security; you need to be sure that access to your Web site doesn't provide a weak link to the often priceless information within your company. Usually, protection involves creating a Firewall to protect the network from unauthorised access. Costs can be high for setting up a corporate

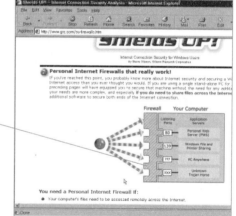

Web site. The benefits can also be enormous or trivial. Arguably, this depends largely on the seriousness of planning and approach.

Creating a Web success plan

'Make a plan, or plan to fail'; those already in business have probably heard this advice many times. For a Web site, it's even more true! Make a Web business plan (initial set-up) and a Web marketing plan (day-to-day planning). Here's the most important requirement for any Web business: make your site look AND perform in an absolutely professional manner. Over deliver on expectations and you'll stand out!

Doing business: an activity checklist

For online stores in which inventory plays a key part, selling wares profitably is crucial to success. To get a better feel for what's involved in providing goods or services from a Web page design standpoint, let's take a brief look at a typical checklist covering the entire transaction process:

When thinking about the design of your pages, take a look at what your competition are doing. This doesn't mean copy their Web content, but it does at least let you know what you've got to beat to 'steal their thunder'.

1 Research and establish the potential market demand for specific products and services on the Web (search engines).

2 Create the design layout for all Web pages. *(Remember: the design of the Home/Index page is particularly important.)*

3 Create the entire text and marketing content for each Web page.

4 Prepare the graphics and integrate them with Web page designs. Possibly include multimedia and animation content.

5 Make it easy to carry out business transactions (for example: design dedicated online forms).

Some Web stores may not even need an inventory. When a customer orders, the Web store contacts its supplier who can send the goods direct to the customer.

6 Set up a reliable, secure way to accept payment for goods or services (ideally use a secure server to process credit card transactions).

7 From the final designs, convert all content to HTML format and test, test, test before going live. Get opinions/feedback.

8 Publish pages to the Web. Do a 'Grand Opening'. Send carefully tailored press releases to all interested parties.

9 Make it easy for people to find your Home page (search engines, press releases, secondary advertising, etc.)

10 Promote your site like crazy for at least 6 months to get established. Then ease off, but keep promoting.

The first 60 seconds!

Many people now live in a 'push-button' society. We like instant results and these reactions are transferred to the Web: we don't like waiting. So the first 60 seconds after a visitor enters your Web site address can make or break its success. As mentioned elsewhere in this book, first impressions do count on the Web. So why not work with this reality; aim to surprise and delight new visitors.

For left-to-right readers, the higher up the page you place your ezine (email newsletter) subscription box, the more likely subscribers are likely to see it, possibly leading to more sign-ups.

Key point: the ideal location is at the left uppermost area of your Web page.

The most important point is to keep the Home/Index page download time to a minimum. If you can do this so that a site loads in under 10 seconds using a 28.8 modem, wonderful! However, under 25 or 30 seconds – or even more – may be tolerated if perceived expectations are high. Aim to deliver on those expectations to keep a new visitor!

Installing an ezine subscription box

For a business, the most important purpose a Web site can fulfil is to capture targeted email addresses. Please reread the previous sentence as it is so important. The first aim is not necessarily to make a sale, although of course no one turns those down.

The point about an email address is that, without it, you can never have a second chance to sell a product or service.

When someone who knows the product or service you're providing leaves an email address, there's a good chance that this person is a hot prospect for what you're offering. If he or she signs up to receive an email newsletter, or regular updates, special offers, or whatever, you have repeated chances to sell. You also have a high level of control over the sales sequence.

Building credibility and trust

Recent statistics from this site – www.Internet Day.com – suggest that 64% of current online sales are abandoned before being completed. Don't be amongst these: make your order process simple, reliable and trustworthy.

'Only scam and con artists sell on the Web' – an untrue phrase but one that with over-hyped media exposure creates great Sunday reading! Web shoppers are the most cautious buyers. To succeed as a respectable Web site owner, you have to fight the false but common misperceptions among the global general public and prove yourself. After all, why should they trust you *before* they get to know you? Actively and regularly show honesty and integrity to gain the trust of visitors. To help think up ideas, let's take a brief look at some positive reasons why people do buy on the Web.

Evaluating why people buy over the Web

People buy from a Web store for many reasons. However, often there's *one important reason above all others* which affects their buying decision. From a Web page design standpoint, we could benefit by identifying some of the more important reasons why people are motivated enough to complete the buying process from a Web store. Consider:

Although businesses can address the 'open 24 hours' issue using answering machines and automated voice systems, it's well known that customers can become irritated with automated replies, possibly leading to lost sales.

• Price, quality, branding, usefulness.

• Perceived value.

• Some folks can simply be so entranced by a Web presentation they buy through impulse mood.

If you can meet that last condition above, you'll be envied by peers and competitors alike – it's the hardest one to achieve.

Guidelines that help build a great reputation

1 Create a Web Privacy policy and Terms of Business page. Make sure visitors know about it and have easy access to it.

2 Protect your visitors' email addresses and other personal details and make it known in several places that you do this. If you say you don't share this information with other parties, stick to your claims: demonstrate integrity.

3 Use a secure server to handle Web credit card transactions. More about this important topic later in this chapter.

Developing a theme-based approach

Nicholas J Schmidt from www.profitstream.com suggests a business approach that, at first, seems to be counter productive for maximum sales, yet nevertheless is a compelling idea.

He suggests that a Web site designed around a fairly narrow theme or idea tends to draw visitors who are more targeted, more likely to buy and more 'pre-qualified'. This approach deliberately attempts to filter out visitors who may be just browsing or curious or just looking for something for free (none of which contribute to sales).

A Web site reflects the company as a whole. A 'bad' Web site therefore can undo years of previous successes – or worse!

So the total number of visitors may be fewer, but of those a higher percentage would probably buy something at some stage. Then, with highly relevant content, great offers and a compelling call to action, you can get more sales!

Club- or business-oriented Web sites often include a variety of Web pages. Navigation for visitors can be made easier by applying a frame-based design to the Home page and including an array of buttons.

This hugely successful Web site sells mobile phones and their accessories

Assessing the competition

For a theme-oriented Web page (or any other Web page) to stand out from the crowd, you need to know just what the 'crowd' is doing on their Web sites. Therefore, with a list of competitors' Web sites prepared, use your Web browser and see how the competition does it:

- Note down the kind of Web page components that gain your attention and try to define why.

- Also, note down those components and elements that irritate you or cause problems for your browser. This kind of information could be useful in establishing what not to include in your own Web pages.

Using doorway pages

A doorway or hook is a Web page you create (containing a carefully crafted individual title, META description and META keywords – Chapter 13) that only links to the 'main' Web site Home/Index page. The 'main' Home/Index pages should not contain any links that point back to any doorway pages. You submit doorway pages to the search engines in the normal way. Doorway pages can only be 'seen' by the search engines, not by visitors, and that's the point: they're designed to increase your exposure to the search engines.

If you decide to use doorway pages, use them with consideration and always abide by search engine rules and regulations.

A power strategy

Here's a potentially highly profitable, perfectly reasonable, ethical strategy that could provide maximum value from the search engines if you have some spare funds available.

Instead of having just a single domain name, get several, all similar if possible. Install your Web site on each and set up links between them all, so that each domain 'points' to each of the others. Modify the content of each Web site if you have a range of product/service lines and try to group each single product or service into a single domain. Make your content concentrate on that product or service only.

Doorway pages can work best when they point to different products/services on multiple Web sites/domains in which each Web site concentrates on a single product or service.

Such doorway pages can almost act like a mini Web site – and therefore are more likely to be 'accepted' by search engines.

Let's see how this could work. Imagine you have 8 domain names/Web sites with about 10 pages in each site. Now add about 30 doorway pages as described above to each site. So each site now has about 40 pages over 8 domains giving you 320 pages working for you in the search engines/directories. Compare that to your original 10 pages with a single Web site!

Why is the number of pages so important? Part of the ranking mechanism in many search engines is how many other pages link to a Web site: 320 pages linked together probably rank better than 10 pages. It's that simple!

Creating doorway pages

You can create doorway pages manually, or using your Web submission/design software. NetObjects Fusion users can purchase www.coolmaps.com MultiDoor Component to automate the task, saving many hours.

Implementing the 2-Step plan

Effective Web pages can be created in many ways. However, you can often make the job easier by constructing and following a basic plan. For example, why not:

Setting up an effective Web site has got to be good for business. However, a poorly maintained Web site can pull the stature of an existing business down surprisingly quickly.

1 Create your Web site with quality as the criteria above all else in mind. Aim for *quality* in all aspects and especially in your information and its presentation.

2 Then, look for ways in which you can *add extra value*, but make sure these are tangible; something that really matters to your potential customers.

Step 1 above is self-evident and is achieved simply through care, consideration and plenty of testing. Real world examples for meeting the Step 2 condition are covered in various sections in this book. However, other ideas for Step 2 could include the following:

Selling a product or service? Why not present brief details of the core subject (don't overload visitors) with 'click' access to lots of backup information using links. Provide this information in a clear, unbiased, sober and factual way using examples where possible.

• Create a virtual hook by providing genuinely valuable free information or key advice to your target audience.

• Include plenty of options for customer feedback.

• Create a 'What's New' or 'Latest Freebies' page.

• Provide a link to your company newsletter (printable).

This popular site provides lots of savvy Internet marketing information for free

Using profit-creating 'magic' words

Words can sell your product or compel a visitor to contact you by phone, fax or person-to-person. Words are powerful, but recent statistics indicate that five times as many people read headlines as read the body copy! Carefully combining headlines with associated graphics and layout can essentially sell your product. The rest is support or detail material.

So what do we want from headlines and body copy? Answer: to grab their attention! You can do this using strong, powerful action-motivated words and phrases. Consider the following guidelines:

 Showing how or why something is the way it is, is more credible than simply telling someone it's better because you say it is! In this way, you're stating your case with evidence instead of simply delivering an online speech.

1 Your headlines are crucial to your success. Include *a strong benefit that is relevant to your visitors* and which makes them stop whatever they're doing and be compelled enough to just want to discover more now!

2 Consider using the three top power words: YOU, NEW and FREE – the most powerful attention 'getters'.

3 Consider including other emotive action words and phrases like: Absorbing, Absolutely, Advice, Amazing, Announcing..., At Last..., Bargains, Boom..., Breakthrough, Compelling, Convincing, Discover, Do You..., Easy, Energising, Fascinating, Finally, Growth, Guarantee, Hate, Health, Here, How much..., How to..., How would..., Interesting, Last Minute..., Love, Luxury, Money, Obsession, Only, Protect, Proven, Results, Rewards, Safety, Sale..., Save, Secrets of..., Security, Share, Show me..., Starter Kit..., The Truth Of... Unique, Useful, Valuable, Yes....

4 Experiment. Keep records of the results you get. Think very carefully before changing a successful headline just because you think it's time for a change.

5 Create compelling reasons *why visitors should buy now*, not later. Make time-dependent offers; be seen to stick to them.

Providing incredible value

To entice visitors to log on to a Web page *and* to keep them coming back repeatedly requires a special kind of thinking. Firstly, when visitors log on to a Web site, remember they're spending in at least three ways:

- The time needed to visit a Web site.

- The time lost through not performing other activities whilst online.

- The cost involved in setting up a Web browser and in maintaining an Internet link (online costs).

Visitors therefore must feel they're getting value from their Web surfing investment. One way to meet this need is to be seen to be providing extra value. *Key hint: find the one thing that makes your organisation absolutely unique and build on it like crazy in your Web site!*

Use 'Show' not 'Tell'. Don't tell visitors how your company can benefit them; show them how and why instead. Example: use verifiable testimonials from previously satisfied customers (but get permission first).

Experiment with ideas: test, measure & modify

Here are some real-world examples. Consider:

- An online music store could provide some free downloads (resolve copyright issues first though).

- A bookstore could give away a free choice of book up to a certain value when a customer places an order above a specific quantity or order value.

- A consultant or market research organisation could provide free information sheets covering key advice on specific topics. This is probably better done using an autoresponder rather than a Web page, so you can capture valuable targeted email addresses.

- An accountancy Web site could provide some free information on a range of topics. Perhaps change the topic once weekly/monthly to heighten interest.

- Press releases could be provided at strategic times giving up-to-the minute information on new products, services or developments which might be of interest to customers.

Effective advertising on the Web

The Web is ideal for advertising: costs can be much lower compared to conventional media. Advertising space on the Web is not in short supply (yet).

However, to be effective, Web adverts need to be attractive, relevant, compelling, clear and quick to load to the following groups of Web user:

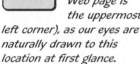

One of the most influential positions on a Web page is the uppermost left corner), as our eyes are naturally drawn to this location at first glance.

- Information seekers.

- Individuals who are cost-conscious.

- Number seekers: those who benefit from viewing statistics, graphs and charts.

- People who are more likely to be motivated to action through a graphically rich Web design environment.

- Those who are first and foremost quality conscious and value oriented.

- People who particularly enjoy audiovisual content.

If your organisation has received positive press coverage, why not refer to this information in a Web site? Respected independent praise can be a powerful sales aid.

One of the most powerful techniques in advertising is to use animation or movement embedded within an eye-catching colour scheme. Web multimedia – the combining of text, graphics, animation, video and sound – makes maximum use of this powerful combination in progressive advertising.

This BT Internet page includes a range of direct advertising and Ad links

Guiding visitors with a Web site tour

If you're providing a Web site tour, create drama; make an impact; stimulate your visitors' imaginations with pleasing sights and sounds.

Evoke the other sensations of touch and smell by drawing on memorable experiences. Relate your message with carefully crafted words as discussed on other pages in this chapter.

For any Web site to be a success, it needs to be actively AND consistently promoted at every opportunity using conventional channels. Try to think of ways in which you can apply this advice to your specific situation.

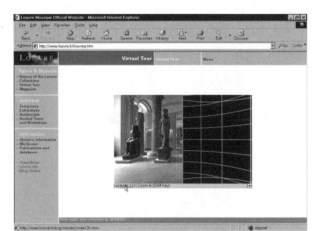

The Louvre museum amazing virtual tour!

Spend as much time as you need to present your content well and leave a lasting favourable impression. Most importantly, put over clearly the benefits you're providing. The closing sequence is an ideal time to fire the imagination and prompt your visitors to action: perhaps to order a product, leave an email address, fill in a form, or revisit specific pages.

The importance of branding

Many experts agree that a strong brand name promoted equally strongly on the Web pages provides one of the most essential ingredients for achieving a successful Web trading experience.

For smaller companies or organisations, it's arguably better not to give the impression of being a large corporation. Web users will probably see through the fabrication eventually and credibility is then lost forever. Instead, why not magnify your impact by using your most powerful asset: your uniqueness, and build on it.

Designing your business Index page

A Web business needs to convert a browsing prospect into a paying customer for as long as possible. Keeping a business-oriented Web site up to date with fresh new content added regularly is *essential* to create an interesting, attractive and dynamic experience for visitors. The Home/Index page is the best place to start.

Avoiding reputation melt down

For businesses and organisations, the Home/Index page is the online equivalent of the front door or corporate reception area. The impression created by an Index page in the mind of a new prospect is crucial to your Web success. A poor or ill-considered corporate Index page can damage an organisation's reputation quicker than most other ways.

If you include links to other Web sites, ideally place these links at another dedicated location (page) to reduce the risk of visitors leaving your Web site erroneously or before you want them to leave.

People make judgements about the business from what they see (and possibly hear) on your Web pages, as well as from what other people may say. It's crucial, therefore, that a business oriented Web site must favourably reflect the image of the company or organisation and the branding of the products and services it represents.

The power of a commercial Home page

The hyperlinks installed in a commercial Home page can provide the key to fast information access. A well thought out Home page can provide visitors with the means to make product comparisons and evaluations, check prices and place orders in minutes instead of hours or days.

A Home page also acts like a signpost, guiding visitors to the desired part of your Web site. The pointers, therefore, need to be clear, easy to use and direct.

However, one of the most striking characteristics of a Home page is that your visitors always keep control. In a conventional sales presentation, only after the recipients have listened to the entire presentation can they decide what is especially useful. Using the hyperlinks in a Home page, however, visitors can navigate to the areas that interest them almost immediately. This fact has powerful implications from a Web design standpoint.

Here's some ideas of what to include in your Index page:

- Business title: individual or organisation name and logo – essential.

- Contact details: postal address, phone and fax numbers; email and Web addresses.

- Copyright statement: essential to protect your work.

- A clear index to your site. Perhaps a graphical toolbar-type design approach, or a 'looser' pictorial graphic design, or something entirely different.

Consider placing a special button or icon (for visitors to click) that allows them to quickly insert the email address of someone they know who would also be interested in your site. In fact, why not maximise this opportunity: consider creating space for up to 5 additional friends or other email sources?

- Links to other pages in the Web site: What's New; Products; Services; Email contacts; etc.

- Links to relevant and thorough information about what you're offering (provide plenty of background information to support your case, but do so in such a way that visitors can choose whether to view it).

- If you want to provide a dedicated Web form page, ideally include a link to it here.

- Why not include something particularly relevant, eye-catching or stimulating to your visitors, and which can be changed or updated as desired? Example: an eye-catching 'What's New' or 'What's Hot' link.

- If relevant, why not include a brief company mission statement or a personalised quote from the managing director, chief executive or other leader?

- Possibly include a link to some genuine and verifiable testimonials from satisfied customers – but get their written permission first. If possible, display a recognised seal of trust icon too.

- A link pointing to job openings within the company.

Competitions, prizes and quizzes

Many of us enjoy competitions. But even if we're not competitive, we might like to have a chance at winning a prize. Competitions, draws, quizzes and so on help add special value to a Web site.

The value of contests

Consider the points below in relation to your Web pages:

Web page crosswords or similar puzzles can help keep visitors interacting with your Web site — and possibly buying an additional product as something particularly relevant 'catches' their eye.

- Contests can urge people to want to visit and revisit.

- Idea: aim to integrate your product or service as part of a contest. In the 'Who did it' style, you could spread strategic 'clues' throughout your Web site to encourage visitors to almost subconsciously take the 'fast track' to learn what's on offer.

Anything new on your Web site, whether it be a contest, new product range or service, should also be promoted further using traditional means like press releases, brochures, and so on.

- Ask contest participants to provide information about themselves. Targeted information is one of the main benefits of hosting a contest. Unless someone shouts their name, you don't know they exist! Anything that encourages visitors to say 'Hello, I'm here, this is who I am and what I like' has real commercial value.

Analysing why visitors revisit

- To gain something for free or to save money.

- The Home page has been bookmarked in the visitor's browser. (Always tell visitors to bookmark your page.)

- There's a compelling interactive component: an online game or perhaps relevant stimulating puzzles.

- To solve a problem, make their job, task or role easier or improve the quality of their life.

- A belief that they are, in some special way, taking part in something bigger, more important than their normal day-to-day activities. The experience of visiting makes them feel good about themselves, by being invited to perhaps contribute in some way or to simply help others.

- The site/page is considered by peers to be 'cool'.

Introduction to E-commerce

Profiling Web page visitors for business

For anyone selling goods/services on the Web, it's essential to learn more about Web users. Visitors who buy online prefer to do so for several different reasons. For example:

Setting up a Web site to take orders can be both a benefit and a shock! Web businesses are open to a global market 24 hours a day, 7 days a week, all through the year. So you need to be sure that your business can cope with this increased level of exposure.

- They like to keep control of the transaction.

- They don't like the hard sell approach.

- They don't appreciate uninvited sales attempts.

- They prefer to purchase when they're ready.

- They like to be assured they can change their mind without penalty.

- They usually prefer to have access to plenty of relevant background information.

- They may not appreciate uninvited email.

Getting ready for E-commerce on your Web site

If you want to handle money on your Web site, for secure transactions your Web host must support Secure Socket Layer (SSL) and handle online forms. Different providers use different scripts to handle this kind of information so discuss these aspects at an early stage.

For large corporate users, considering setting up a Web site is a particularly important step. If you host the entire operation in-house, costs can be high.

As transaction-type Web pages involve considerably more technical and design input, they can cost more to develop. However, new easy-to-use software packages or E-commerce 'plug-ins' are now available. For example, see: www.floyd.co.uk/ and www.vi.net/ – ideal for small and medium businesses to handle Web transactions easily.

Corporate Web transactions

When considering the business of Web transactions, the same advice as provided on the opposite page for small businesses also applies to corporates. However, arguably the demands and risks are greater so you need to be sure everything works securely and correctly.

NETBANX

Web credit card transactions

Any business faced with the task of setting up a Web-based display of products with access to a secure ordering facility normally requires access to people with skills in database programming, installing a database on a secure server, and ensuring high security applies in the areas of product viewing, ordering and performing transactions.

The Web is part of a fairly new landscape. In this ungoverned land, the rules are hazy at best. Any business wanting to create a Web presence should make detailed plans and exercise caution when forming new online partnerships or alignments.

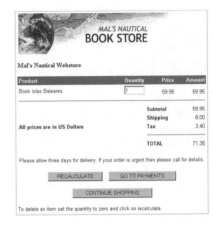

Lots of different shopping cart systems are now available for Web businesses. For example, Virtual Internet's SnapSell software (http://www.vi.net/) helps make the job much easier. Other free and low-cost shopping cart options are also available through companies like Mal's E-commerce (http://www.mals-e.com) through which you can set up your online shop to accept secure credit card payments in a range of currencies.

You can design a Web page form to send its information using 'standard' email. However, the information is not as secure when compared to using a CGI script. Especially avoid using 'standard' email when sending sensitive data.

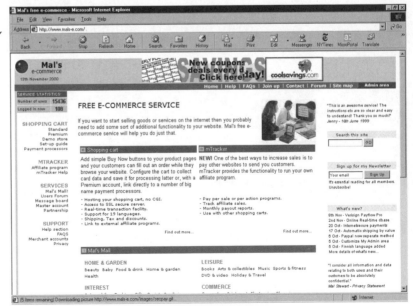

Online security: using secure servers

Sending sensitive information like credit card details over the Internet and the Web has been given a massive boost recently by the popular application of secure servers. A secure server is a powerful PC which encrypts sensitive data to keep it private and highly secure.

Here's how to easily identify a secure server: look at the Web address; If there's an 's' as in https://, the link is secure.

(Ordinary Web addresses start with: http://)

When conventional credit card transactions take place in, for example, a restaurant or retail store, unscrupulous individuals can simply listen carefully and look over a payee's shoulder to gain quite a lot of useful information.

Not so with a secure server! Web transactions carried out through reputable organisations with secure servers are now probably one of the safer ways to pay for goods and services – and the public are coming to realise this as PCs and the Web become ever more commonplace.

What exactly is a secure server?

You can easily tell if you're connecting through a secure server in Netscape Navigator browsers: look at the key icon situated at the lower left of the screen. This key appears in unbroken blue for secured connections and broken blue for unsecured links.

A server is simply a powerful PC which serves other PCs in a special way. The 'secure' description implies that information moving between the central server and the PCs it serves is protected in some way: usually this is done by encrypting the information to deter unauthorised access.

Why bother providing a secure server?

When sensitive information like credit card details are transferred on the Internet without protection, key information can be used to steal from the credit card holder's account. Although Internet buyers now have better protection from most good credit card companies, a secure server offers better security.

Protecting privacy with encryption technology

The best secure servers use the Secure Sockets Layer (SSL) system. SSL is an encryption technology available on Microsoft Windows and Apple Mac platforms. Technical info: SSL can use a 128-bit encryption key for US transactions and a 40-bit (or larger) key for international transactions. SSL is really bad news for prospective Internet thieves.

Autoresponders: your 24-hour tool

Make email work for you. Failing to reply to an email is like setting up an 0800 number and then ignoring the phone when it rings.

On the Web, folks are impatient and first impressions count, so it's especially important that you respond quickly and efficiently to enquiries. Answer: autoresponders – one of the most powerful Web tools available. An autoresponder (or infobot) is an automated email-type fax back system. When someone sends an email to you or to a Web address you specify, your autoresponder replies automatically usually within seconds or minutes. Smart autoresponders can now be set to follow up on previous messages several times.

Working 24 hours a day even when your PC is switched off, an autoresponder sends your marketing information to potentially tens of thousands of people across the globe. Autoresponders can also be set up for lots of different purposes. Discover more: type 'autoresponder' into your favourite search engine. Consider the following points:

Email offers superb value for money! If you're in business, why not (after completing a sale and obtaining payment) email a separate 'Thank you for your order' message to your customer immediately or definitely within a few days? Or, better still, use an autoresponder to do it for you.

- An autoresponder can provide a valuable time-saving element by being designed on a FAQ (Frequently Asked Questions) basis.

- With autoresponders, you can quickly ensure most questions are answered promptly and properly.

- With careful design, visitors may not even be aware that they have received an automated response.

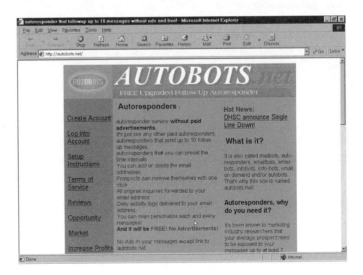

Designing a Web page order form

Doing business on the Web is not that different from trading using the traditional routes. On the Web, you can:

- Display products and services attractively.

- Take orders effectively and process them promptly.

- Dispatch or deliver the product or service.

- Cause customer interaction/feedback *(this maintains a bond with existing clients & builds future business).*

In this section, though, we're concentrating on the second item above. A Web page order form usually comes into play as soon as a visitor clicks on a 'How to Order product' button, or something equivalent. Consider:

When crafting the text content for a 'Cancel order' button, don't forget to relate this to any Sale of Goods laws that may apply in your country, state or area, if necessary.

1 Clearly define the process through which visitors can choose your products or the services you provide.

2 Translate each stage of this process to components in an order form. If you're dealing in products, consider attaching a 'Buy this' button (or equivalent) next to each product.

3 Design a form so visitors know what to do every time. Keep instructions brief and simple. Make meanings clear.

A 'Cancel Order' option can provide less wasted time for you as the vendor, and shows you've invested time and consideration in addressing how to deal with simple mistakes to the benefit of all.

4 Provide a 'Cancel Order' option (see margin tip) to apply before and after an order has been given within reason.

5 Ask a few carefully selected testers to test your form to ensure it is easy to use and works properly.

6 Consider including a link to your order form on every page.

7 Integrate the HTML form with scripting components if necessary. Discuss these aspects with your Internet Service Provider, especially during the early stages of your designs to avoid wasting time later.

Ensuring you get paid

Getting paid is of course crucial whatever methods you use to deliver your product/service.

If you're involved in a business which is not totally Internet-based, then you probably already have several established payment options.

But what if you want to set up a system to accept payments through your Web pages?

There's a lot of silly hype surrounding e-commerce. If a credit card call back system works profitably for you, then question why you should spend more time and money trying to change it.

There are several ways of getting paid over the Internet; probably the best, quickest and safest is payment by credit card using a secure server as examined on previous pages. However, for purchases of less than about £5, this method is probably not cost effective.

Providing payment choices: some current options

Not everyone wants to – or can – pay by credit card online. Remember, a huge group of younger or teenage buyers may not yet have access to their own credit card, yet might be prepared to buy if a suitable alternative were available. This group has money to spend so why not just provide a range of payment alternatives?

One approach is to design your page to prompt visitors to enter specific details of their order and their contact information including telephone and email addresses if available. Then provide your customer with some payment choices, such as the two options below:

- Option 1: here the customer can omit credit card details but include specific contact telephone and fax numbers. Explain that once a customer hits the 'Send' button, a representative will contact them shortly to take down credit card details over the phone.

- Option 2: Ensure that order information and credit card details can be printed out and sent by fax or mailed to the desired payment address.

An example: how Dell does it

A lot of money can be made on the Web, but it's not suitable for every single business (just most). The product, branding and the strategy have to be right from the start.

Let's take a brief look at one company that has been hailed by many as an icon for successful trading on the Internet: Dell computers. Currently, Dell takes online orders for thousands of PCs each day. In 1998, almost 30% of Dell's total sales came from online purchases.

However, when we look a little closer, we can see that Dell's position is arguably more unusual than most on the Web. One could say that setting up their online store was easy. Consider the following points:

If you're in business and intend to sell products and services from your Web site to other countries in the EU, find out about the EU Distance Selling Directives, to determine how they might affect you – especially those dealing with VAT.

- Before starting up a Web presence, they already had an impressive IT infrastructure established.

- They already traded on a global scale.

- They had been dealing directly with the public for some time before setting up their online presence.

- The techniques, and to a certain extent, the experience, were already established, at least in part.

So for Dell, we could perhaps say the Internet and Web represented a natural progression, an evolutionary development, rather than a completely new venture.

These same arguments – with a little creative thinking – could perhaps apply to many other types of organisations. For example, banks and retail stores – especially those selling computer software, books or music products.

Perhaps this is one reason why many businesses in these categories have made successful transitions to the Web and appear to be promoting themselves well on the Internet.

The key point is that any individual, club, business or organisation can make true assessments of strengths, weaknesses, opportunities and threats (SWOT test) in relation to providing a possible presence on the Web.

Launching, promoting and marketing

In this final chapter, we examine the sometimes tricky business of publishing a Web site. We also reveal powerful key techniques to promote and monitor your Web site through the search engines, newsgroups and mailing lists.

Covers

Chapter Fifteen

Prelaunch checking and testing

Once your Web design is complete, don't upload it to the Web until you've thoroughly tested it using (ideally) several browsers. To maintain credibility, it's important to test and re-test every aspect before publishing to the Web.

Make a checklist to log your progress

Putting Web pages together effectively involves a surprising variety of skills. It's easy therefore to make simple errors in spelling, create incorrect grammar or use incorrect or dead URLs, and so on. Consider these steps:

1 When your Web pages are almost complete, consider creating a checklist to prevent 'howlers' getting through.

2 Then check all the Web pages for only one type of fault in your list. If you see other types, resist the temptation to be swayed: you'll pick up those faults on the next cycle.

3 Here's an idea of what to check: spelling, grammar, punctuation, layout, dead URL links, style consistency, links, download times (especially graphics) and animation.

4 Even after carrying out steps 1, 2 and 3 above, mistakes can still occur. Consider asking another person to check your work using these steps as a guide.

More about CuteFTP at: www.cuteftp.com/

Uploading your Web site

When you're ready to upload or publish your Web site to the Web, you can use FTP (File Transfer Protocol) software, sometimes called an FTP client. FTP software comes:

Software demos, free copies and updates are often available on the CD-ROMs that come with popular computer magazines.

- As part of existing Web design software. Examples include: Adobe GoLive, Microsoft FrontPage, NetObjects Fusion, Macromedia Dreamweaver.

- As a separate application. CuteFTP and FTP Explorer are two excellent examples. FTP Explorer is currently free for non-commercial use (www.ftpx.com/) and CuteFTP is shareware (www.cuteftp.com/).

Time-saver: whatever FTP software you choose, ensure that it allows you to publish updates or changed pages in addition to regular publishing. Consider the following guidelines:

To compel visitors to keep re-visiting, continually add new and fresh content to your site. Consider ways to separate your site from the crowd. Promote your uniqueness!

1 Make sure the format you use for your Web page filenames is correct for the Web host you're using. Many Web hosts use the computer language UNIX and INDEX.HTML, Index.htm and index.html may not be considered the same. Also, check that you're using correct filename extension; examples include: .html, .htm, and .shtml

2 When your Web host allocates you Web space, you should also receive 4 pieces of essential information: (1) the exact Web address to which you upload your site – example: ftp.yourcompany.com or even just www.yourcompany.com, (2) Your username, (3) Your password, (4) the address (base directory) of the folder to which you upload your site; example: /usr/www/yourcomp/html or simply 'html'

3 If your site uses Web forms, you may need to know the full Web address that points to the cgi-bin for your site.

4 Read your FTP or publishing documentation. Upload your site. Start your Web browser and view your new Web site.

Introduction to searching the Web

What is a search engine?

A search engine is a continually updated folder made up of hundreds of thousands or millions of Web pages. Search engines use powerful PCs or 'spiders' that continuously visit Web pages to record information including all related links they can find and other information for possible inclusion in their databases. Usually, the more links a Web site has pointing to it, the higher it ranks in a search engine's database. Search engine examples include Alta Vista (www.altavista.digital.com/) and InfoSeek (www.infoseek.com/).

What is a directory?

A directory lists Web sites in logical categories. To get listed, usually you need to submit your Web site details to the directory and a human operator, rather than a search engine spider, decides whether to list your site. Examples include: Yahoo (www.yahoo.co.uk/) and YELL, the Internet Yellow Pages (www.yell.co.uk/).

Using the search engines and directories

The Web can be likened to a vast unordered library in which new books appear continuously, other books disappear and others may seem to 'move' around without warning. Search engines and directories help make sense of this apparent chaos.

Although powerful, search engines and directories are usually easy to use: simply enter the words or phrase you want, then click the 'Search' or 'Send' button. However, to filter out irrelevant data, learn as much as possible about using relevant search engines and directories. Metacrawlers like www.dogpile.com and www.go2net.com query several search engines at once for what you want.

The trick is to think of precise words that you want to look for, *not* descriptions or concepts relating to what you want. Also, think of alternatives. For example, people in the UK who want to search for 'Football' should remember that this represents American football in the USA; the answer is to enter 'Soccer' as well.

Downloading files from the Web can take a long time. If your Internet connection is broken, you have to download the file again. To save your sanity, choose a product that can resume downloading from where you left off.

Consider GoZilla (currently free) www.gozilla.com/ or GetRight (www.getright.com/).

Your Web submission strategy

So now you're at the stage of completing your Web page design and have uploaded or published your pages to the Web. Congratulations! One of the quickest and easiest ways of letting others know about your Web page is to register it with as many search engines as possible. For maximum impact, register your Web page on each and every search engine that you know of. However, a small number are the most important (see overleaf). Consider these guidelines:

1 In your Web browser, enter the site submission Web page address for the search engine/directory you want.

2 (Optional) If necessary, choose the option referring to 'registering a new Web site'.

3 Enter your Web site details. Usually, you can enter the name of your Web site or page, your Web and email addresses and other basic contact details. If you're prompted to enter keywords and a description, consider these carefully: refer to the guidelines given at the start of Chapter 13.

4 When complete, 'Submit' your details to register your Web presence. You'll then probably receive an email message about your request: keep it for your records.

If you don't want to spend time registering your Web page with multiple search engines, companies are available online who will do it for you. For example, you could try: http://www. submit-it.com

Yahoo's 'Suggest A Site' page

Choosing promotion search tools

You can submit your Web site to hundreds of different search engines and directories. However, 95% of your Web traffic will probably come from just a few.

The current search engine and directory submission Web addresses are shown in brackets. Even though these may change without notice as the providers update their services, if in doubt, simply go to the Home/Index page and look for the new link.

Yahoo is arguably the most important directory for a Web business to get listed. However, as Yahoo uses people to evaluate Web sites before including them, it's now not easy to get into Yahoo.
   Consider submitting through local versions of Yahoo, like yahoo.co.uk/ instead of yahoo.com/

The most important search engines:

- **Alta Vista** http://www.altavista.digital.com/
  (http://www.altavista.com/cgi-bin/query?pg=addurl)
- **AOL NetFind** http://search.aol.com/
  (http://search.aol.com/add.adp)
- **Excite UK** http://www.excite.co.uk/
  (http://www.excite.com/info/add_url)
- **Google** http://www.google.com/
  (http://www.google.com/addurl)
- **GoTo** http://www.goto.com/
  (Keywords can be purchased. Contact address above)
- **HotBot** http://www.hotbot.com/
  (http://www.hotbot.com/addurl.asp)
- **InfoSeek** http://www.infoseek.com/
  (http://www.go.com/AddUrl?&pg=SubmitUrl.html)
- **Lycos** http://www.lycos.com/
  (http://www.lycos.com/addasite.html)
- **Lycos UK** http://www-uk.lycos.com/
  (http://www-uk.lycos.com/service/addasite.html)
- **MSN Search** http://www.search.msn.com/
  (http://www.search.msn.com/addurl.asp)
- **Northern Light** http://www.northernlight.com/
  (http://www.northernlight.com/docs/register.htm)
- **Search** http://www.search.com/
  (No submit area: search results come from InfoSeek)
- **WebCrawler** http://webcrawler.com/
  (http://www.webcrawler.com/info/add_url/)

Directories:

- **Magellan** http://www.mckinley.com/
- **Open Source Directory** http://www.dmoz.org/
  (http:/www.dmoz.org/add.html)
- **Real Names** (& submit) http://www.realnames.com/
- **Yahoo UK** http://www.yahoo.co.uk/
  (1. Navigate to category, 2. Click 'Submit a site' link)
- **Yell** – http://www.yell.co.uk/

Search engine secrets revealed

1 When considering words/phrases for a Web search, note several perhaps complementary words/phrases that could point to what you want. Example: if searching for *global warming*, also try *ozone depletion.*

2 For best results, re-submit your Web site(s) to the search engines at least once every 4-6 weeks. Why? Search engines regularly update their listings to seek new content.

3 Don't resubmit your Web site URL too often: some search engines penalise sites that re-submit every day for example. You could consider resubmitting a different hook page every day or two, but do check the search engine rules first.

4 Read the site submission rules for each search engine before submitting your site. For best results, manually submit your site to each search engine one at a time rather than using 'basic' site submission software or services.

5 Try to get listed in the Inktomi search engine database. Inktomi currently drives HotBot, GoTo and Yahoo. A submission form is available at www.hotbot.com/

6 At GoTo.com, you can bid for and purchase keywords that visitors might use to find your Web site. This approach could be profitable and worthwhile! To discover more, visit: www.goto.com/

Your Web site is like a tiny island in a huge ocean, so getting noticed is the main objective – especially for business Web sites. Getting a high ranking in a search engine even on a single keyword can bring huge numbers of visitors to your site!

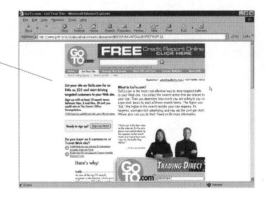

High search engine positioning

Get your Web listed in the first 30 search returns

Imagine: create a highly valuable information product worth at least 5 or 6 times what you sell it for. Guidelines given in your information product can immediately recover the cost of the product 6 times over. You don't want to be greedy so you sell it on your Web site for a reasonable £20.

Assume your Web site now generates 50,000 hits/month. Only 3% decide to buy; 3% of 50,000 gives us 1500 x £20 = £30,000. Multiply that by 12 (months) = £360,000 p/year. Imagine your Web site development + ongoing costs are £5,000. Your products's total annual development + ongoing costs = £10,000-£20,000. So your grand total outlay is £25,000 maximum. Annual profit = £335,000.

 Although this example can make the job look easy, it's not. A lot of hard work, re-work and constant promotion is usually required. Also, the search engines and directories continually change their ranking rules. Nevertheless, software like WebPosition Gold can help you keep up-to-date.

The key to this not uncommon level of success is the number of hits a Web site generates. *People only visit and revisit a Web site that offers them a strong reason to visit!* Something free, valuable, which saves them money, helps them earn more money, etc. Key areas include: money, love, health, food, travel and gaining knowledge or skills.

When people use search engines, even though their search may return hundreds or even thousands of possible Web sites, most view only the first 30 or so links. Your goal is to get your Web site as high as possible within the first 30 returns for a particular search word or phrase.

If you can achieve this far from easy task, your Web site traffic, or number of visitors or hits, will probably soar to incredible heights! If you apply the techniques outlined in this book successfully, a proportion of visitors will buy.

The key: effective and thorough search engine positioning software

WebPosition Gold (WPG) software can help ensure your Web site is placed high in the search engines. WPG contains 7 key modules: Page Generator, Page Critic, Upload Manager, Submitter, Reporter, Scheduler, Traffic Analyser. You can download a (currently free) demo from FirstPlace Software at: www.webposition.com/

Web site promotion: top tips

Those who are serious about Web site positioning/ ranking should check their Web site's position regularly.

Powerful submission software like WebPosition Gold can help make the job much easier.

To gain most from your Web pages, you need to actively promote them both on the Web and off-line. There are several ways in which you can do this; your choices depend on whether your Web pages are business oriented or more for personal or hobby use. Consider these guidelines:

1. Seek out complementary Web sites; both parties could benefit from cross-linking. Email the Webmaster and put your proposition.

2. Create a benefit-packed email signature; consider the guidelines provided on the following pages. Ensure your email software includes this signature on all emails you send.

3. 'Register' or broadcast your Web site correctly with the key search engines and directories as discussed in this chapter.

For businesses, Web cards could be worth considering as part of a promotion project. Web cards are about the size of a post card and contain a picture of your Web site Home page on one side and other key details. Ideal for special offers, etc.

4. If you're in business, use traditional routes for advertising your new Web site. Create a compelling press release. Tip: gain an editor's attention using an unusual topic, theme, problem-solving or human interest angle. Then send this to a range of carefully selected promotional sources.

5. Newsgroups and mailing lists can provide another avenue of promotion – if used with consideration. People who share a common interest or have something to say can post articles; start and take part in discussions; seek help to solve a problem; and announce something new. Caution: first read the guidelines provided later in this Chapter.

6. People like quizzes, contests and promotions! By hosting and regularly updating something appropriate like this, you can interact more with your visitors to stimulate and maintain further interest in your Web pages.

Tapping the full power of email

Effective use of the Internet can make business communications easier and cheaper. The telephone is clearly much cheaper than designing, producing and sending a letter. But sending an email is cheaper still: one reason why over 400 million emails are sent across the globe each day. Try to integrate email communications closely with your Web page designs to fully benefit.

Some browsers include email built in. However, for more power and flexibility, you can use separate email software. Two popular applications are Eudora (www. qualcomm.com) and Pegasus Mail (www. pegasus.usa.com/)

Email: formatting for maximum impact

To ensure the maximum number of recipients can read and see your email message properly, keep to plain text (ASCII) format (not HTML). If possible, avoid using indents, tabs and justified alignments. Set the word wrap at about 65 characters to reduce eye strain on your readers. Just type your message using simple 4- or 5-line paragraphs. When you enter a Web or email address, your email software may automatically underline it in blue to show it's a hyperlink.

Using domain email formats

If you have a 'true' domain like: yourcompany.com, you can create a range of professional, effective and easy to remember email addresses. Consider:

Currently, Microsoft Outlook Express email and news reader comes free with Internet Explorer. Outlook Express allows you to set up multiple email Signatures.

orders@yourcompany.com
support@yourcompany.com
quiz@yourcompany.com
help@yourcompany.com

So when anyone sends an email to one of these addresses, you immediately know what the email is about.

Creating powerful, compelling email signatures

An email signature is a brief text message (ideally under 7 lines) that automatically accompanies any email message you send. For businesses, an email signature is a kind of business card. Most email software includes commands to set up email signatures; See your email guide for details.

You could include essential contact information: (optionally, your name, postal address, telephone/fax numbers and email/ Web addresses). Your email signature can be formal or friendly and you can create several different types for use for different purposes. For businesses, consider also including a slogan or brief but striking benefit-packed phrase describing something important, relevant, or new linked to a Web/email address.

Experiment with email signatures. You can also include special characters top and bottom to 'frame' the text content. Just remember signatures that are seen as too long, too wordy, or just too pushy can do more harm than good. Sometimes, a 'soft-sell' approach stands out better.

Microsoft Outlook 2000: a superb personal organiser and email program, here showing the 'Welcome' message in HTML format

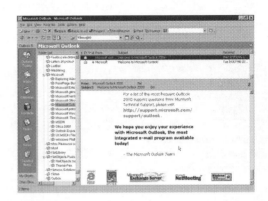

Example 1: general soft-sell email signature:

Brian Austin MISTC
computer author, trainer, IT support specialist.
e: b.austin@mycompany.com
w: http://www.mycompany.com

Example 2: a more business-oriented signature:

brian@internettips.net
http://www.internettips.net/
http://www.post-master/rs/internettips
http://www.marketingtips.com/t.cgi/12939/

Wow! Want to earn income online in 45 countries? Send me an email with: 'Want to earn income online' in the Subject.

PS: Have a great day!

When sending an email to a newsgroup, you can modify it as below to prevent automatic scanners capturing your email address and sending you unwanted mail.
  Example: j.smith(NOSPAM)@ jstop20.com (remove NOSPAM before replying).

Example 3: a powerful, benefit-packed signature:

John Smith
http://www.js-top20.com/
Your Web site in the Top 20, or your money back!
Call toll free now: + 44 0800 123456

Marketing through the newsgroups

A newsgroup is a computer-based storage area containing a collection of articles or posted messages on a particular topic. Newsgroups and mailing lists are simply the Internet equivalent of clubs. Over 40,000 different newsgroups and mailing lists exist covering thousands of different topics.

People who share a common interest or have something to say can post articles, start discussions, seek assistance and announce something new. Anyone can post to a newsgroup and anyone can read newsgroup postings. Newsgroups can be accessed through the Internet using a News reader, like the currently free Outlook Express from Microsoft.

Avoid blatant and repeated unsolicited advertising of any products or services to ensure that you don't anger other newsgroup members.

Promoting a product or service to a newsgroup

Promotion of a product/service is possible through some newsgroups and can be effective although many don't tolerate 'open' commercial advertising. *Key point: be seen to be putting the needs of other members before your own.* Solve a problem! Offer free advice! Be genuinely helpful and many newsgroups will tolerate a link to your Web site that is part of your email signature – included when you contribute in the newsgroup.

Free Agent is another excellent news-reader. Currently free for non-commercial use: www.forteinc.com/

Having said that, many companies and organisations do break the unwritten rules. This approach can invite more problems for the 'unofficial law breaker' than it solves. Sometimes warnings may be sent to the perceived offender before action may be taken – which might include spamming or flaming (repeated high volume emails to an email address).

Microsoft Outlook Express email and Newsgroup reader

Newsgroups: top tips

1 If you're considering posting an article, make up a list of all the relevant newsgroups. You can usually download all the newsgroup titles available to you through your dial-up connection from your Internet Service Provider.

Regularly taking part in newsgroups is one of the fastest ways to get a lot of (probably unwanted) email. Some people may 'gather' or harvest email addresses from newsgroups without the users' permission, then add the email addresses to a mailing list and sell it to other parties for another round of 'spamming'.

2 Avoid using your 'real' email address: consider using a format similar to that in the HOT TIP on page 181. Why? See the tip on the left. Or consider getting and using another email address: some generous providers like Microsoft's Hotmail service (www.hotmail.com) can provide free email addresses.

3 Before contributing to a newsgroup, watch how others submit and answer questions and note what level of advertising is 'tolerated'.

4 If you're still unsure, email the Sysop or newsgroup administrator direct and ask about the rules.

5 Design an appropriate message. Keep it simple, brief and to the point. Make a useful contribution.

6 Post your message in all the *relevant* newsgroups. However, don't send your message to more than five newsgroups at any one time: if a newsgroup becomes saturated, your message may become lost and recipients may become irritated by the excessive repetition (spamming).

7 If you break the rules by mistake, apologise as soon as possible but never reply to personal email insults or flames.

Using mailing lists

A mailing list and a fax broadcast are simply different versions of the same thing. With an opt-in email mailing list, you can contact tens of thousands of people across the globe who have previously given their permission to receive your information, for a relatively small cost. The cost of sending and receiving email is tiny compared to fax and conventional mail.

However, most of these lists are to allow people to share information, skills, solutions and ideas freely. Anyone wanting to sell goods and services on a regular basis shouldn't consider mailing lists as the main avenue of business. Mailing list contributors can react very negatively against those blatantly carrying out 'excessive' commercial activities.

You can find mailing lists using the Internet search engines and at mailing list directory sites such as: http://www. reference.com/

If you're in business, you can use mailing lists to generate useful contacts, sales leads and eventually income. For best results, you can create your own 'ezine' mailing list.

Although no laws exist to stop companies advertising in the mailing lists, a lot of grief can be avoided by respecting the right to privacy of individuals against excessive commercialism. Although mailing lists are not really designed with commerce in mind, brief commercial details included at the end of a useful message are usually tolerated, provided these details are discreet.

Also, if the contribution received by the participants in the list is perceived to be especially valuable and worthwhile, news about such contributions can be spread quite quickly. Carefully crafted email signatures as discussed on previous pages can reap benefits far in excess of the amount of input required to create them.

Utilising your Web statistics

A good Web host provides additional services other than just Web space. Some can log the number of 'hits' to your site and also provide demographic data such as where your visitors are located and so on. For businesses, this represents hot information! WebTrends is one particularly powerful tracking software used; if your Web host does not already have this installed, ask if they'll install it for you to use.

The www. coolmaps .com Site-Reporter Component for NetObjects Fusion 4.x users can calculate essential statistics like upload time and typical browser download times, and check links and images.

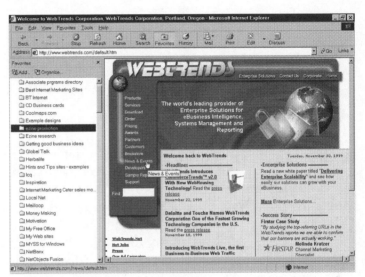

The WebTrends web site at www.webtrends.com/

Some Web design software can work with plug-ins that monitor your Web designs to help identify problems before you publish a site to the Web.

Using unique reply references

If you're providing some interactive element in your Web site, like quizzes or prizes, here's another way to test your Web page response. You can invite people to reply to your address, stating a unique reference number along with the other information you're requesting.

You'll then know respondents could only have seen this reference on your Web site. Using these kinds of approaches, you can build a profile of who your contacts are, where they live, what their interests are, and so on.

Some final thoughts

Maintaining the momentum

To make a Web site really work, it's not a bad idea to pretend that it's never finished. In other words, to encourage new visitors and prompt previous visitors to return, plan to actively promote and publicise it regularly.

Consider the following pointers to help you devise new ways to encourage visitors to return:

- Regularly look for ideas to generate schemes which you think would appeal to your visitors.

- Find your visitors' 'Hot' buttons i.e. learn what they really want from your Web site and try to provide it.

- Try to find ways of interacting with previous visitors. For example: if you have previously obtained an individual's date of birth details, you could email birthday congratulations several days before the event with no strings attached, other than simply mentioning the Web page and inviting your customer to revisit. You could perhaps even include a mention of birthdays on the Web site. However, consider this carefully; remember, some people may be sensitive about their age being revealed openly.

- Update a static Web site. Perhaps bring in multimedia, Flash- and ActiveX-type components to help provide the illusion of fresh, new, exciting active content. Also, consider publishing genuine updates through traditional avenues, press releases, etc.

Why not use this book as your 'personal Web success workbook'? Highlight relevant parts, mark pages and scribble your own notes in the margins. With just a little extra work applying the techniques in this book, you could recover your small investment thousands of times over – and why not?

A personal Thank You

Thank you for buying and using Web Page Design in easy steps. I know there's a lot to think about in this book – that's where the value lies! You can take your time. Work at your own pace, doing a little every day to achieve your goals. Or you can get serious and set yourself ambitious targets. Most of all, have fun! Don't be afraid to make mistakes – everybody else has at some stage – just learn from them and move on. Now why not go and make your mark – or your fortune – in Cyberspace. Think big and good luck!

Index

h

i

j

l

m

n

o

p

q